BASE BALL PLAYER'S

BOOK OF REFERENCE.

A BASE BALL FIELD.

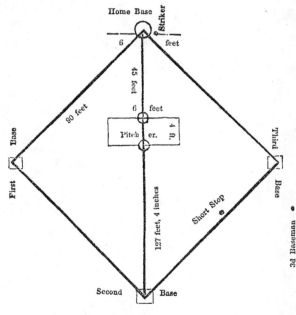

Catcher

Scorers

Umpire

Home Base   Striker

6   feet

45 feet

6   feet

4 ft.

Pitcher

90 feet

First   Base

Third   Base

First Baseman

3d Baseman

Short Stop

127 feet, 4 inches

Second   Base

Second Baseman

Right Field

Centre Field

Left Field

THE

BASE BALL PLAYER'S
BOOK OF REFERENCE.

CONTAINING

The Revised Rules of the Game for 1867,

WITH AN

EXPLANATORY APPENDIX TO EACH RULE, TOGETHER WITH
FULL INSTRUCTIONS FOR UMPIRES AND SCORERS, AND
ALSO FOR PITCHING, BATTING AND FIELDING.
THE WHOLE FORMING A STANDARD

Authority on all points of the National Game.

By HENRY CHADWICK,

Of the Committee on Rules of the National Association; and Base
Ball Reporter of the Principal New York Weeklies.

1867.

Published in cooperation with
The Henry Ford

APPLEWOOD BOOKS
CARLISLE, MASSACHUSETTS

The Base Ball Player's Book of Reference, The Revised Rules of the Game for 1867, was originally published by J. C. Haney & Co. of New York.

This edition is reproduced from the original in the collections of The Henry Ford, Dearborn, Michigan.

Thank you for purchasing an Applewood Book. Applewood reprints America's lively classics—books from the past that are still of interest to modern readers. For a free copy of our current catalog, write to: Applewood Books, P.O. Box 27, Carlisle, MA 01741

ISBN 978-1-55709-595-4

20 19 18 17 16 15

Printed in Canada

PREFACE.

THE necessity for some standard work on the rules of base ball, more extensive and explanatory in its character than the Book of the National Association, has long been felt by the fraternity; and to supply this want was the intention of the author of the BASE BALL PLAYER'S BOOK OF REFERENCE, which work was first published in July, 1866. The idea was to make the book the standard authority on all the points of the game, and inasmuch as the author of it has been engaged in reporting the leading base ball contests of the metropolis and principal cities of the country for the past ten years, and, as a consequence, has been a close observer of the practical working of the several rules, besides, as a regular member of the Committee on Rules for several years, having been prominent in bringing the game up to its present high standard of play, it naturally follows that he should be regarded as a reliable authority for the settlement of disputed points in reference to the correct definition of the rules, and, also, in regard to the best method for a full development of the skill of a player in the three departments of the game, viz: pitching, batting and fielding. As proof of the estimation in which the author's opinion on all matters appertaining to base ball is held, it is but necessary to refer to the fact, that every doubtful point, on which a decided opinion was ex-

pressed, in the first edition of this work, in reference
to any particular definition of the rules, the opinion
of the author was fully indorsed at the Convention
of 1866, and all his suggestions adopted with scarcely a dissentient voice, and that, too, at the most
largely attended and influential meeting of the National Association ever held. The publishers regard
it as but simple justice to the author to mention
these facts, and by way of indorsement of the state-
ments made, they take occasion to present the following complimentary certificate from the able Committee on Rules of the National Association for 1866:

NEW YORK, December 12, 1866.

To THE BASE BALL FRATERNITY AT LARGE:

We, the undersigned, members of the Committee on Rules and
Regulations of the National Association of Base Ball Players, having known Mr. HENRY CHADWICK as an experienced and impartial
reporter of the game for the past ten years, and having been asso-
ciated with him in the Committee on Rules, of which he has been
a prominent member for several successive years, hereby indorse
him as a competent authority on all questions appertaining to base
ball, and, especially, as an author of commentaries on the rules of
the game; and we heartily commend his existing publications on
base ball as standard works on the subject. We, also, specially
recommend his last work, entitled THE BASE BALL PLAYER'S BOOK
OF REFERENCE, as a book that should be in the hands of every member of the fraternity. (Signed.)

J. B. JONES, M. D., President of the Excelsior Club, Brooklyn;
and Chairman of the Committee.
PETER O'BRIEN, of the Atlantic Club, Brooklyn.
D. W. C. MOORE, President of the Athletic Club, Philadelphia.
WM. H. BELL, M. D., President of the Eclectic Club, New York.
A. P. GORMAN, President of the National Club, Washington.
THOS. G. VOORHIS, President of the Empire Club, New York.
CHAS. E. THOMAS, of the Eureka Club, Newark.
MORTIMER ROGERS, of the Lowell Club, Boston.

HANEY & CO., PUBLISHERS,
119 Nassau Street, New York.

INTRODUCTION.

THE NATIONAL SPORTS OF AMERICANS.

THE physique of Americans has long been a vulnerable point for the attacks of foreigners on the weaknesses of our countrymen, and hitherto we have only too-well merited the palpable hits made by our healthy out-door-sport-loving cousins of England. Of late years, however, an improvement has been manifested in this respect, in America, and a reformation has been introduced, which bids fair to remove the cause of complaint, and to bring us up to the physical standard of our forefathers, whose well-exercised muscles enabled them to lay low the forests of the Western wilderness, and whose powers of endurance led them to withstand so manfully the fatigues and trials of the great seven years' struggle for independence.

Among the most influential causes of this desirable reformation has been the establishment of a NATIONAL OUT-DOOR SPORT, something we were not possessed of even so late as ten years ago. Of course our sports must necessarily be, in the main, of foreign origin, as are the sports of England of Norman or Roman descent; but we can as fairly claim for our American game of Base Ball—as played in accordance with the rules of the "National Association of Base Ball Players"—an orginality as an American institution, as the

English people can for their peculiarly national sport of the Fox Chase. Without further discussion on this point, however, let it suffice that the game of Base Ball, as perfected of late years, is, undoubtedly, an American game, and one we can now fairly claim as our national out-door sport.

What Cricket is to an Englishman, Base Ball has become to an American. In England, Cricket has more devoted admirers and more ardent followers than any recreation known to the English people. On the Cricket field—and there only—the Peer and the Peasant meet on equal terms; the possession of courage, nerve, judgment, skill, endurance and activity alone giving the palm of superiority. In fact, a more democratic institution does not exist in Europe than this self-same Cricket; and as regards its popularity, the records of the thousands of games played each year, which include the names of Lords and Commoners, Divines and Lawyers, Legislators and Artizans, and Literateurs as well as Mechanics and Laborers, shows how great a hold it has on the people. If this is the characteristic of Cricket in aristocratic and monarchical England, how much more will the same characteristics mark Base Ball in democratic and republican America?

Unreflecting and prejudiced individuals, who never look beneath the surface of things, may regard both Cricket and Base Ball " as very good things for boys, perhaps," or to "pass away an idle hour or so on a holiday;" but those who intelligently investigate subjects in regard to cause and effect, see in both these games, but especially in Base Ball, the means to an end which has been sought for in vain for years past, on this side the Atlantic. As a means of cultivating the physical powers, Base Ball is one of the most commendable exercises in vogue. As a remedy for many of the evils resulting from the immoral associations the boys and young men of our cities are apt to become connected with, the game merits the indorsement of every clergyman in the country; and we are gratified to notice that one eminent preacher has publicly commended Base Ball from the pulpit, the Rev. C. H. Everett, of Brooklyn, in a sermon he delivered in 1865, on Physical Education, having made a special allusion to Base Ball as a game "whose regulations are calculated to prevent the ill-feelings engendered by other games, and one, moreover, which serves to attract our young men from places of bad repute, and to supply in place thereof the right kind of recreation and exercise." This opinion has been indorsed by several clergymen of Philadelphia, who, the same year, formed themselves into a Base Ball Club for purposes of moral and healthful recreation, in imitation of hundreds of their brother clergymen of England, who take such delight in playing Cricket with their parishioners on the "commons" or "greens" of the villages, over which they have pastoral control.

But one of the strongest aids to the popularity of Base Ball, lays in the fact that it is a game—and about the only one, by-the-way—which can be countenanced and patronized by the fair sex. American ladies have hitherto been shut out from all the pleasures incident to games, in which contests are entered upon for the palm of superiority in courage, activity, nerve, judgment and manly skill, by the low character of the surroundings of most of the sports and pastimes men indulge in. In Base Ball, however, we have an exception in favor of the ladies, and one, too, they have not been slow to avail themselves of, as the presence of the fair sex by hundreds at a time at the leading contests of the past five or six seasons fully testifies. If our National Pastime had no other recommendation than this, this alone would suffice to give it a popularity no other recreation could reach or compete with, in the estimation of Americans. To conclude our introduction, however, we have to state that whether Base Ball be regarded as a desirable means of physical exercise, an exciting game for the masses, a recreation for the refined classes of the community, or an out-door sport devoid of every objectional attribute to the most fastidious moralist could charge it with possessing, it is equally to be commended to the patronage of every reputable citizen, North, East, South and West, as the most suitable game for the national out-door sport of the American people.

The following is the attitude of the pitcher when about to make the last swing of the arm in delivery.

In delivering the ball the arm can be bent at angle, but not outward from the body; when so bent in delivery it must hang perpendicularly.

THE

BASE BALL PLAYER'S

BOOK OF REFERENCE.

The Ball.

SEC. 1. The ball must weigh not less than five and one-half, nor more than five and three-fourths ounces, avoirdupois. It must measure not less than nine and one-half, nor more than nine and three-fourths inches in circumference. It must be composed of India rubber and yarn, and covered with leather, and, in all match games, shall be furnished by the challenging club, and become the property of the winning club as a trophy of victory.

[In selecting a ball for a match, the one nine and one-half inches in circumference, and five and three quarters ounces in weight, will be found the most elastic, and the best for batting purposes, because the yarn and rubber in it is wound tighter than in balls measuring more and weighing less. It will be seen that the rule makes it incumbent on the *challenging* club to furnish the ball on each occasion of a match game.]

The Bat.

SEC. 2. The bat must be round, and must not exceed two and a half inches in diameter in the thickest part. It must be made of wood, and may be of any length to suit the striker.

[The lighter the bat, provided the wood is of a tough kind, the better. It is almost impossible to hit quick enough for swift pitching with a heavy bat, unless the batsman is very strong in the arms. Strength in the wrists is the main thing in batting.]

The Bases.

SEC. 3. The bases must be four in number, placed at equal distances from each other, and securely fastened upon each corner of a square, whose sides are respectively thirty yards. They must be so constructed as to be distinctly seen by the umpire, and must cover a space equal to one square foot of surface. The first, second and third bases shall be canvas bags, painted white, and filled with some soft material, the home base and pitcher's point to be each marked by a flat, circular iron plate, painted or enameled white.

[There have been several patent-bases introduced, those used on the Union ball grounds, Brooklyn, being the best. As a general thing, the canvas bag strapped round the centre with a strong leather band will be found as serviceable as any. The rule makes the base-bag the base, not the post to which it is fastened.]

The Home Base.

SEC. 4. The base from which the ball is struck shall be designated the Home Base, and must be directly opposite the second base; the first base must always be that upon the right hand, and the third base that upon the left hand side of the striker, when occupying his position at the Home Base. And in all match games a line connecting the home and first base and the home and third base, shall be marked by the use of chalk, or other suitable material, so as to be distinctly seen by the umpire.

[It is very necessary that the rule in regard to having chalk lines made, should be enforced, as it greatly assists the umpire in deciding on foul balls, besides making it plain to all present that the decisions are correct. The home-base quoit should be *flat*, as the rule requires, and not rising in the centre, as some do; for when a ball touches the latter, instead of rebounding for the catcher, as it would do if the base were flat, it flies off at a tangent, and allows of bases being run on the passed ball.]

The Pitcher's Position.

SEC. 5. The pitcher's position shall be designated by two lines, two yards in length, drawn at right angles to a line from home to second base, having their centres upon that line at two fixed iron plates, placed at points fifteen and sixteen and one-third yards distant from the home base. The pitcher must stand within the lines, and must deliver the ball as near as possible over the centre of the home base, and fairly for the striker.

[The term " fairly for the striker " means balls pitched within his legitimate reach—that is, the length of his bat from him—and not balls which the striker's whim or fancy may call for. If the batsman is in the habit of striking a very low or very high ball, then the pitcher must pitch the ball to suit his peculiar style, viz.: " fairly for the striker; " but he is not required so to pitch unless the batsman is in the habit of striking at balls of the kind, or in other words, the batsman cannot demand a low ball if he is in the habit of striking one hip high. The change in the rule is the reduction of the line of the pitcher's position from twelve feet to six, and requiring none but fair balls to be delivered to the batsman. Before, the striker could call for any ball he liked, fair or unfair; now, he can only demand one pitched to the point he has been in the habit of striking from, and not where he may want it for a special purpose.]

Delivering Unfair Balls.

SEC. 6. Should the pitcher repeatedly fail to deliver to the striker fair balls, for the apparent purpose of delaying the game, or for any cause, the umpire, after warning him, shall call one ball, and if the pitcher persists in such action, two and three balls; when three balls shall have been called, the striker shall take the first base; and should any base be occupied at that time, each player occupying it or them shall take one base without being put out. All balls delivered by the pitcher, striking the ground before reaching the line of the home base, or pitched over the head of the batsman, or pitched to the side opposite to that which the batsman strikes from, shall be considered unfair balls.

[Before balls are called on a pitcher, he must be warned by the umpire; but only one warning is necessary for each striker. If two balls are pitched unfairly, after such warning, then " one ball " should be called, and if after that, one unfair ball be delivered, then " two balls " and " three balls " should be called. A little latitude should be allowed in the first innings, but not afterward. A pitcher " repeatedly " fails if he fails twice in succession; and he " persists " in his unfair delivery if he pitch one ball after the first penalty has been imposed. By the rule as amended the umpire is now obliged to call every ball a " ball " if it be delivered as above described. The only discretionary power he has in the matter, being in regard to balls " fairly for the striker," this class of balls being left to the umpire's judgment. No " ball " however must be called unless the pitcher has first been warned, one warning for each striker being sufficient.

Pitching.—Balks.

SEC. 7. The ball must be pitched, not jerked or thrown, to the bat; and whenever the pitcher moves with the apparent purpose or pretension to deliver the ball, he shall so deliver it, and must have neither foot in advance of the front line or off the ground at the time of delivering the ball; and if he fails in either of these particulars, then it shall be declared a

balk. The ball shall be considered as jerked,
in the meaning of the rule, if the pitcher's arm
touches his person when the arm is swung forward to deliver the ball; and it shall be regarded as a throw if the arm be bent at the elbow, at an angle from the body, or horizontally
from the shoulder, when it is swung forward to
deliver the ball. A pitched ball is one delivered
with the arm straight, and swinging perpendicularly, and free from the body.

[A "pitched" ball is one that reaches the batsman
without touching the ground. If it touches the ground it
becomes a "bowled" ball. A "jerked" ball is a ball delivered swiftly from the hand by the arm first touching the
side of the pitcher; if the arm does not touch his side the
ball is not "jerked." A ball can be thrown under hand
as well as over the shoulder; but it cannot be thrown with
a straight arm. Therefore, if the pitcher keeps a straight
arm, that is, without bending his elbow, he does not throw
the ball. The sentence, "time of delivering the ball," has
been interpreted by the Committee on Rules and Regulations of the National Association, to mean the period when
the last movement of the arm is made in delivering the
ball; and, consequently, if either foot of the pitcher be off
the ground when this movement is made—it being nearly
simultaneous with the ball leaving the hand of the pitcher
—umpires must declare a balk without being appealed to.
The amendment simply defines a jerk, a throw and a legitimately pitched ball, and by this means the umpire is relieved
of the responsibility he had to bear last season.]

Rules for Players when a Balk is Made.

SEC. 8.   When a baulk is made by the pitch-

er, every player running the bases is entitled
to one base without being put out.

[The striker cannot take a base on a balk for the reason
that he is not a player running the bases until he has
struck a fair ball.]

A Player Running the Base.

SEC. 9. The striker shall be considered a
player running the bases as soon as he has
struck a fair ball.

[This is a new section, and it was introduced for the
purpose of removing the confliction of the rules on this
subject which previously existed. Now the striker is only
considered the striker until he has struck a fair ball; before he was considered the striker until he had made his
first base.]

Balked and Called Balls are Dead.

SEC. 10. Any ball delivered by the pitcher
on which a balk or a ball has been called, shall
be considered dead and not in the play until it
has been settled in the hands of the pitcher,
while he stands within the lines of his position;
and no such ball, if hit, shall put the striker
out.

[This is also a new section and a very necessary amendment. It should be understood that no bases can be given
the striker on any dead ball he hits, for the same reason
that prevents him taking a base on a balk, viz: that he is
not a player running the bases until he has struck a fair

ball, and balked or called balls are not fair balls.   This rule however does not affect section 6 at all.   (*See Appendix.*)

Foul and Fair Balls.

SEC. 11.   If the ball, from a stroke of the bat, first touches the ground, the person of a player or any other object, behind the range of home and the first base, or home and the third base, it shall be termed foul, and must be so declared by the umpire, unasked.   If the ball first touches the ground, the person of a player or any other object either upon, or in front of the range of those bases, it shall be considered fair.

[Special rules are requisite in all cases where there are peculiarities of a ground to interfere with fielding operations, such as a tree, a house or a fence in the way.   In such cases, if a foul ball is caught on the fly from a tree, it counts only as a bound catch, and if a fair ball is held on the fly on a re-bound, from a fence or a house, it is no catch unless mutually agreed to be so considered before the game is commenced.   If a ball strikes the hand or person of a fielder, fairly, and re-bounds outside the line of the bases it is nevertheless a fair ball.   And if it strikes the fielder's person outside the range of the bases and rebounds to the ground inside, it is still a foul ball.   A fielder however, may be standing within the line and yet reach out to catch the ball in such manner as to have his hand make the ball foul by touching it outside the range of the base line.]

Making the Home Base.

SEC. 12.   A player making the home base shall be entitled to score one run.

[Home runs are not recognized by the rules. Custom considers a home run as being made, if the home base is reached before the ball passes the line of the home base from the outer field, provided the batsman has not been obliged to stop on any base to avoid being put out. A "clean home run"—and none other should be counted in the score—is a run made from home to home, from a hit made to long-field beyond the reach of the out-fielders.]

Balls Struck at and Missed.

SEC. 13. If three balls are struck at, and missed, and the last one is not caught, either flying or upon the first bound, it shall be considered fair, and the striker must attempt to make his run.

[The Committee of Rules have decided that the bound catch in this instance shall be considered in the light of a foul ball, as far as the catch is concerned, from the fact of its striking the ground back of the home base.]

A Foul Ball Caught puts the Striker Out.

SEC. 14. The striker is out if a foul ball is caught, either before touching the ground, or upon the first bound.

[If a fair or foul fly ball is missed by one fielder, and another catches the ball from his hands or person before it touches the ground, such a catch counts as a fly catch; and in the case of a foul-bound ball being similarly missed by one fielder and caught by another, it is regarded as a fair catch. But if in the latter case it be caught re-bounding from the person of any one not engaged in the game as a fielder, then it does not count.]

Striking Out.

SEC. 15.   Or, if three balls are struck at and missed, and the last is caught, either before touching the ground, or upon the first bound, provided the balls struck at are not those on which balls or balks have been called, or not those struck at for the purpose of wilfully striking out.

[This rule as amended, now places an obstacle in the way of players, who are mean enough to "play the game into the dark," as it is called. Scorers should record the batsman as "struck out" in this instance, whether he is caught out by the catcher or put out at first base after the bound catch has been missed.]

A Fair Ball on the Fly.

SEC. 16.   Or, if a fair ball is struck, and the ball is caught without having touched the ground.

[A tree, a fence, or a building, are all regarded as "the ground" in this instance, and if the ball touches either before it is caught, the catch does not count, except in the case of a foul ball when a fly ball touching a tree &c., becomes a bound ball, but it must be taken on the fly from the tree or object it strikes.]

Ball Held by Adversary,

Sec. 17.   Or, if a fair ball is struck, and the ball is held by an adversary on first base, before the striker touches that base.

[It should be distinctly understood by all that the ball must be held by the base player with some part of his person on the first base, " before " the striker touches it, or he is not out ; if, at the same time, he is not out. It must be palpable that the ball was held by the base player before the base was touched by the base runner or the latter is not out.]

Players touched by the Ball while Running.

Sec. 18.   Any player running the bases is out if at any time he is touched by the ball while in play in the hands of an adversary, without some part of his person being on the base.

[A player makes his base if he touches the base-bag, no matter whether the base-bag is in its position or not. That alone is considered the " base." Section 3 states that ",the first, second and third bases shall be canvas bags."]

No Base can be made on a Foul Ball.

Sec. 19.   No run or base can be made upon a foul ball ; such a ball shall be considered dead, and not in play until it shall first have been settled in the hands of the pitcher.   In such cases players running bases shall return to them, and may be put out in so returning in the same manner as when running to the first base.

[The player running the bases must return to the base he left when the ball was struck, and *remain upon it* until the ball is " settled " in the hands of the pitcher, after which he can leave his base.]

Running Bases.

SEC. 20. No run or base can be made when a
fair ball has been caught without having touched the ground, such a ball shall be considered
alive and in play. In such cases players running bases shall return to them, and may be
put out in so returning, in the same manner as
the striker when running to first base; but
players, when balls are so caught, may run
their bases immediately after the ball has been
settled in the hands of the player catching it.

[In the case of fair balls taken on the fly, a player,
running his bases when the ball is struck, must return to
the base he left, and touch it, and wait on it until the ball
is settled in the hands of the fielder catching it; after
which he can again run for the next base without waiting
for the ball to go to the pitcher; but in the case of foul
balls the base runner must stand on his base until the ball
is settled in the hands of the pitcher. The only change in
the above two rules is the substitution of the word " run"
for " ace."]

SEC. 21. The striker, when in the act of
striking, shall not step forward or backward,
but must stand on a line drawn through the
centre of the home base, not exceeding in
length three feet from either side thereof, and
parallel with the line occupied by the pitcher.
He shall be considered the striker until he has
struck a fair ball. Players must strike in regular rotation, and, after the first innings is play-

ed, the turn commences with the player who stands on the list next to the one who lost the third hand.

[This standing on the line of his position is quite important. In the first place the striker has no right to avail himself of the advantage derived from standing back of the line of his position, thereby increasing the distance between himself and the pitcher and obtaining a better opportunity of judging the ball; besides which, a poorly hit ball which would strike the ground in front of the home base—if the batsman stood on the line of his base—and lead to his being put out, is changed to a foul ball by his standing back of his base, and he thereby escapes the penalty of his poor batting. Another fact is, the striker, by not standing on the line in question, deprives himself of the right to demand fair balls from the pitcher. The amendments to this rule include one preventing the batsman from taking the privilege of making a step forward to gain impetus for striking, or a step backwards to increase the distance between himself and the pitcher; and also one to define how long he shall be considered the striker.]

Vacating Bases.—Putting Players Out.

SEC. 22. Players must make their bases in the order of striking; and when a fair ball is struck, and not caught flying, the first base must be vacated, as also the second and third bases, if they are occupied at the same time. Players may be put out on any base, under these circumstances, in the same manner as when running to the first base.

[Players running bases can only be forced to leave their bases when each base is occupied, and the striker hits a

fair ball.   No player can run another off a base under any
other circumstances.   The only change in this rule was in
taking out the words "the striker" in the last line but
one.]

Bases must be Touched.—Order of Bases.

SEC. 23.   Players running bases must touch
them; and, so far as possible, keep upon the
direct line between them; and must touch
them in the following order; first, second, third
and home; and if returning must reverse this
order; and should any player run three feet out
of this line, for the purpose of avoiding the
ball in the hands of an adversary, he shall be
declared out.

[A player running his bases can only be decided out by
the umpire for running out the line of the bases when he
does so to avoid the ball.   If he does so to avoid interfer-
ing with a fielder, he does not infringe the rule.   If he fails
to touch a base he must return to it, and must be touched
with the ball before he does return, in order to put him
out.]

Preventing a Player Catching a Ball.

SEC. 24.   Any player, who shall intentionally prevent an adversary from catching or fielding the ball, shall be declared out.

Unfair Base Play.

SEC. 25.   If the player is prevented from
making a base, by the intentional obstruction

of an adversary, he shall be entitled to that base, and not be put out.

[The word "intentionally," in these rules, refers to actions which might have been avoided. Thus, if a fielder happens to be standing on the line of a base to catch a falling ball, the player has no right to run up against him because he is between him and the base, for he can run a foot or two to one side and not thereby be prevented from reaching his base by the effort of the fielder to catch the ball. So in regard to a base player taking a ball from a fielder, he having no right to stand between the player and the base when the ball could be equally well taken by standing out of the way of his adversary. In these instances the obstruction should be regarded as intentional, from the fact that it might readily have been avoided.

Stopping the Ball,—Non-Players.

SEC. 26. If an adversary stops the ball with his hat or cap, or if a ball be stopped by any person not engaged in the game, or if it be taken from the hands of any one not engaged in the game, no player can be put out unless the ball shall first have been settled in the hands of the pitcher when he is standing within the lines of his position.

[If the ball be stopped by a crowd at the back of either the first or third base, the ball must be returned to the pitcher before it can be used to put a player out, and it must be settled in the hands of the pitcher while he stands within the lines of his position before it is again in play.]

Striker Out.

SEC. 27. If a ball, from the stroke of a bat,

is held under any other circumstances than as enumerated in Section 26, and without having touched the ground, the striker is out.

[If a ball be held in the lap of a fielder, or between his knees, or on his feet before it touches the ground it is a fair catch. The amendment to this rule prevents the pitcher from leaving his position to take any ball stopped by out-siders in a game. Formerly the rule was nullified by the pitcher running to the base to take a ball stopped by the crowd.]

Running Home after the Striker is Out.

SEC. 28. If two hands are already out, no player running home at the time the ball is struck can make a *run to count in the score of the game* if the striker is put out by a fair catch, by being touched between home and the first base, or by the ball being held by an ad-versary at the first base before the striker reaches it.

[Of course, if the striker makes his first base, and is touched with the ball in trying to make his second base, or either of the other bases, the player running home before him scores his run; but the home base, in such an instance as this, must be reached before the player is put out, or the run does not count. The moment the third hand is out no player running home can count his run if the home base is touched after the player is put out. The amend-ment was made in order that the rule of play should remain as before, viz:—no run being scored by a player running home when two hands are out if the "striker" was put out, the striker then being considered such until he had made his first base. By defining the rule differently, so as not to conflict with other sections, as it did before, the rule of play is made the same, though it is differently worded.]

Innings Concluded when Third Hand is Out.

SEC. 29. An inning must be concluded at the time the third hand is put out.

[Any number of innings can be played after the ninth inning, until one party or the other takes the lead provided the score is even at the close of the ninth inning.]

What Concludes the Game.

SEC. 30. The game shall consist of nine innings to each side, when should the number of runs be equal, the play shall be continued until a majority of runs, upon an equal number of innings, shall be declared, which shall conclude the game.

[Any less number than five innings does not constitute a game. If any number of innings have been played between five and nine, and the last inning is not completed on account of darkness or rain, the result of the last even innings played decides a game. Thus if five innings have been played and one side have played their sixth, and the other side have two hands out on their sixth inning, and it becomes too dark for the umpire to see the ball, or too wet from rain for play to be continued, and the game be "called" by the umpire, the score of the five innings played decides the contest.]

Regulations of Matches.

SEC. 31. In playing all matches, nine players from each club shall constitute a full field, and they must have been regular members of the club which they represent, and of no other club, either in or out of the National Association, for thirty days immediately prior to the match. Position of players and choice of innings shall be determined by captains, previously appointed for that purpose by the respective clubs.

[The above rule does not exclude members of cricket clubs, as cricket is a different game. But it excludes members of all base ball clubs, whether of the senior or junior fraternity, or of clubs in or out of the National Association. No player can be changed, viz : one player of the club not in the nine, substituted for another who is in, unless for just cause, such as positive inability to play by reason of illness or serious injury. Mutual consent cannot permit one player to be substituted for another, except for the causes indicated. Therefore, if any particular player is wanted and he is not on hand at the time the game begins, the side he belongs to must play eight men, or put in a player in his place who must play through the entire game. The only change in this rule was the striking out of the words " no change or substitution," &c., the same being embodied in another rule.] (*See Appendix.*)

SEC. 32. The umpire shall take care that the regulations respecting the ball, bats, bases, and the pitcher's and striker's position are strictly observed. He shall be the judge of fair and unfair play, and shall determine all disputes and differences which may occur during the game.

He shall take special care to declare all foul
balls, balks, strikes and balls immediately upon
their occurrence, and when a player is put out,
in what position and manner, unasked, and in a
distinct and audible manner. He shall, in every
instance, before leaving the ground, declare the
winning club, and shall record his decision in
the book of the scorers.

[The amendments to this rule require the umpire to call
balls and strikes in a loud voice the moment they occur,
and without "judgment" being called. And he must
also, when a player is put out, at once call out, in a loud
voice how and in what position he has been put out without being asked. Thus, if a player be put out on the fly
by the centre fielder, the umpire must immediately call out,
"striker out on the fly by centre fielder." By this means
the scoring of the fielding play will be greatly facilitated.
For complete rules for the guidance of umpire see "Instructions for Umpires."]

Selection of Umpire and Scorers.

SEC. 33. In all matches the umpire shall be
selected by the captains of the respective sides,
and shall perform all the duties enumerated in
Section 32, except recording the game, which
shall be done by two scorers, one of whom shall
be appointed by each of the contending clubs.

[Clubs should remember that no man can act as umpire
in a match without their mutual consent ; and therefore
after having chosen their umpire they should abide fully
by his decisions, and if these happen to be partial the best
way is to keep silent and make a better selection next
time.]

Bets by Umpires and Players Illegal.

SEC. 34. No person engaged in a match, either as umpire, scorer or player, shall be either directly or indirectly interested in any bet upon the game. Neither umpire, scorer or player shall be changed during the match, unless with the consent of both parties, except for reason of illness or injury or for a violation of this law, and then the umpire may dismiss any transgressor.

[The change in this rule is simply the introduction of the words " for reason of illness or injury," in the place of the words " violation of section 29."]

When Play shall be Suspended.

SEC. 35. The umpire in any match shall determine when play shall be suspended; and if the game cannot be concluded, it shall be decided by the last even innings, provided five innings have been played; and the party having the greatest number of runs shall be declared the winner.

[It will be seen from the above rule that the umpire alone has power to suspend the game, the captains having no voice in the matter beyond making suggestions. If the umpire says continue the game, and one side or the other refuse to play, then the game becomes null and void.]

Balls Knocked Beyond Bounds.

SEC. 36. Clubs may adopt such rules respecting balls knocked beyond or outside the bounds of the field, as the circumstances of the ground may demand; and these rules shall govern all matches played upon the ground, provided that they are distinctly made known to every player and the umpire previous to the commencement of the game.

[The adoption of the special rules referred to in this section applies only to rules governing catches made from trees, fences or buildings, the number of bases made on hits over fences or buildings, and these do not apply unless a mutual understanding is had previous to the commencement of the game.]

Communicating with the Umpire.

Sec. 37. No person shall be permitted to approach or to speak with the umpire, scorers, or players, or in any manner to interrupt or interfere during the progress of the game, unless by special request of the umpire.

[The habit that players have of standing talking near the umpire should be put a stop to. The umpire needs all his wits about him to attend to his duties, and everything calculated to distract his attention from the game should be avoided.]

Umpires and Scorers to be Members of a Club.

Sec. 38. No person shall be permitted to act as umpire or scorer in any match unless he

shall be a member of a Base Ball Club governed by these rules.

[This is one of the rules which is seldom observed.
Every club should appoint a regular scorer for the season,
and he should be competent to record the fielding as well
as batting score of the game. Until this is done, a full
analysis of the season's play of a club cannot be obtained.]

Play to be Called at the Time Appointed,

SEC. 39.   Whenever a match shall have been
determined upon between two clubs, play shall
be called at the exact hour appointed; and
should either party fail to produce their players within thirty minutes thereafter, the party
so failing shall admit a defeat, and shall deliver
the ball before leaving the ground, which ball
must be received by the club who are ready to
play, and the game shall be considered as won,
and so counted in the list of matches played:
and the winning club shall be entitled to a
score of nine runs for any game so forfeited,
unless the delinquent side fail to play on account of a recent death of one of its members,
and sufficient time has not elapsed to enable
them to give their opponents due notice before arriving on the ground.

[By the amendments introduced in this rule, clubs are
obliged to enforce the penalty inflicted by the rule for its
non-observance. When clubs appoint a time for calling
the game it should be promptly proceeded with after the
time allowed by the rule has expired.]

Games Considered Null and Void.

SEC. 40. Any match game played by any club in contravention of the rules adopted by this Association, shall be considered null and void, and shall not be counted in the list of match games won or lost, except a game be delayed by rain beyond the time appointed to commence the same. Any match game can be put off by mutual consent of the parties about engaging in the game. No match game shall be commenced in the rain.

[This rule was designed to obviate the difficulty attendant upon the repudiation of any rule of the game any two clubs may mutually agree to ignore. Thus, for instance, any two clubs agreeing to allow a member of either club to play in a match who has not been a member for thirty days previous to a match, by this rule cannot claim the ball won, or count the match played as a regular game. The exception made in case of rain refers to that rule which requires a game to commence within thirty minutes of the time appointed.]

What Professional Players Are.

SEC. 41. No person who shall be in arrears to any other club, or shall at any time receive compensation for his services as a player, shall be competent to play in any match. All players who play base ball for place, emolument, or money, shall be regarded as professional players; and no professional player shall take part in any match game; and any club giving any compensation to a player, or having to their knowledge a player in their nine playing in a match for compensation, shall be debarred from membership in the National Association, and they shall not be considered by any club belonging to this Association as a proper club to engage in a match with, and should any club so engage with them they shall forfeit membership.

[This was one of the most important amendments made to the rules in 1866. By it all players, who make ball playing a business, are excluded from taking part in match games between Association clubs. Players who desire to speculate in base ball matches must form professional nines, or otherwise they will not be able to get up a match.]

Failure of the Striker to Strike.

SEC. 42.   Should the striker stand at the bat, without striking at good balls repeatedly pitched to him, for the apparent purpose of delaying the game, or of giving advantage to a player, the umpire, after warning him, shall call one strike, and if he persists in such action, two and three strikes; when three strikes are called, he shall be subject to the same rules as if he had struck at three fair balls.

[Section 42 is a rule that should be strictly enforced, as it refers to a part of the game that is oft-times a very tedious and annoying feature. It is a frequent thing to see the striker, the moment his predecessor has made his first base, stand at the home base and under the plea of not having fair balls pitched to him, await the moment when the player on the first base can avail himself of the failure of either the pitcher or catcher to hold the ball while tossing it backward and forward to each other. In every respect it is preferable to play the game manfully and without resorting to any such trickery as this, which not only tires the spectator, but detracts from the merit of the game itself. Even under the present rule of pitching, this unfair play was practised last season. It is to be hoped that umpires will do their duty this year, and put an entire stop to it, which they have now the power to do.]

What Decides a Match.

SEC. 43. Every match hereafter made shall be decided by the best two games out of three, unless a single game shall be mutually agreed upon by the contesting clubs.

[It should be understood between clubs challenging each other that if the series should not be played out the same season the games played should count as nothing.]

THE POSITION OF UMPIRE.

ITS DUTIES, &c.

THE QUALIFICATIONS OF AN UMPIRE.—It is almost un necessary to remark that the first duty of an umpire is to enforce the rules of the game with the strictest impartiality. An all-important requisite, too, is familiarity with every point of the game. Experience has shown the fallacy of the opinion that because a man happens to be an excellent player, he must necessarily make a good umpire. We have seen too many instances in which almost the very reverse has been the case, to adopt that as a rule. It requires a man of considerable moral courage to act impartially in the position; and decision of character, coolness of judgment and quickness in observation are also necessary qualifications. These several characteristics few possess, and consequently thoroughly competent umpires are to be found few and far between.

SELECTING AN UMPIRE.—In selecting an umpire, choose the man you know to be "a true man," that is, one who, howsoever he may err in judgment, decides a point according to his honest and unprejudiced opinion. Such a one is preferable to any other, who, lacking this quality, possesses every other attribute of a competent judge.

WHO CAN ACT AS UMPIRE.—No man can act as an umpire in a match, who is not a member of a club belonging to the National Association.

FAVORS CONFERRED BY UMPIRES.—Contesting nines and their friends invariably forget, in their comments on the decisions of umpires, that the umpire is the *obliging* party, and the players his debtors. Without an umpire no game can be played; and inasmuch as the position of umpire, in a base ball match, must always be an office unpaid for and honorary in its character, unless all unpleasantness connected with the position, and all objections to occupying it, are removed, it will be difficult to obtain any one willing to assume the office who is worthy and competent to act.

AVOID PREJUDICING AN UMPIRE.—If an umpire commits an error, finding fault with him will not improve his judgment; on the contrary it is very likely to prejudice him against the parties censuring him. The best way, when errors are committed, is to remember that the umpire is doing your club a favor in acting in the position, and to credit him with endeavoring to do his best to oblige. Above all, remember that your captain, as your representative, consented to his occupying the position, and that therefore he is not acting as umpire in opposition to the wishes of your club.

QUESTIONING DECISIONS.—In no case has any player of a nine a right to question the decision of an umpire except the captain, and he only in the form of soliciting information in regard to a disputed point, and not as questioning the umpire's judgment. The captain alone is the spokesman of the nine. If a player should become cognizant of an error of the umpire's requiring explanation, as sometimes occurs, let him call "Time," and point out the error to the captain. This should be done, however, only in rare instances, and where the error committed is a palpable one in interpreting the rules, and not an error of judgment. As a general rule, however, *silent acquiescence* in every decision of the umpire is the best policy, as it certainly is the one most characteristic of gentlemanly players.

THE GOLDEN RULE IN UMPIRING.—The umpire should invariably render his decision in accordance with the *first impressions* of the point of play, made on his mind. If he hesitates at all, the influence of any particular bias he may have will affect his judgment, and very likely make his decision a partial one. Be prompt, therefore, to decide according to the very first impression made. Promptness in deciding is strong testimony in favor of impartial judgment, and is always satisfactory to contestants.

THE DUTIES OF UMPIRES.

WHAT THE LAW SAYS.

" Sec. 32.   The umpire shall take care that the regulations respecting the ball, bats, bases, and the pitcher's and
striker's position are strictly observed.   He shall be the
judge of fair and unfair play, and shall determine all
disputes and differences which may occur during the game.
He shall take special care to declare all foul balls, balks,
strikes and balls immediately upon their occurrence, and
when a player is put out, in what position and manner,
unasked, and in a distinct and audible manner.   He shall,
in every instance, before leaving the ground, declare the
winning club, and shall record his decision in the books of
the scorers."

The Size of the Ball.—Before " play" is called, the
Umpire should see that the *ball*, to be played with, is of
the regulation size and weight, viz., not more than five and
three fourths ounces in weight, nor less than nine and one
half inches in circumference.

The Foul Ball Lines and Posts.—He should also see
that the *Foul Ball Posts* are in position, and especially
that the rule requiring *chalk lines*, from home to first base
and home to third, be complied with.

The Pitcher's Position.—He should also see that the
lines of the pitcher's position are properly laid down, viz.,
forty five feet from the home base for the front line, and
four feet further for the back line; with a line of six feet in
length for the position; and within this space the pitcher
must stand, keeping both feet on the ground, from the time
he prepares to deliver the ball, until it leaves his hand.

The Striker's Position.—He should see that the striker, when he takes his position to strike, has one foot on
the line of his position.   This is a very important rule,

and yet it is one that few Umpires have enforced hitherto.
In the first place, if the striker is permitted to stand two
or three feet back of the home base, and he strikes a ball
nearly perpendicular to the ground, the ball touches the
ground back of the home base and at once becomes a foul
ball, and in such cases the rebound is generally one making
a catch difficult. Now, the very same ball, struck by the
batsman while in his proper position, viz., with one foot on
the line of the home base, would invariably be a fair ball,
and one that would lead to his being easily put out at first
base. It will be seen, therefore, that by not standing on
the line of his position he gains an advantage he is not entitled to. Again, if the striker be not in his proper position, he cannot legally insist upon fair balls being delivered
to him; and as the Umpire is the sole judge of fair and
unfair play, and this failure of the striker to stand on the
line of the position is unfair play, the Umpire should not
inflict any penalty upon the pitcher for failing to deliver
fair balls to him while he is thus out of his place. The
new rule prohibits the striker, when about to strike at a
ball, from either stepping backward or forward. It should
be borne in mind also that the striker is considered the
striker only until he strikes a fair ball, after which he
immediately becomes a player running the bases.

CALLING FOUL BALLS.—He should call foul balls in a
loud tone of voice, especially when a player is running his
bases. When a ball is struck high in the air, and it is
doubtful whether it will fall fair or foul, the Umpire should
wait until the ball touches the ground or the person of a
player before he calls "foul," for until it does so touch
the ground, it really is not a foul ball. When the ball is
"tipped" he can call it foul more promptly than when
struck high in the air.

PROCLAIMING HOW A PLAYER IS OUT.—The Umpire is required when a player is put out to tell how he has been put
out, and by whom. Thus, if the striker is put out by the

second base man on the fly, the Umpire must call out, "striker out on the fly by second base man."

SILENCE FOR FAIR BALLS.—The Umpire should keep silent when a fair ball is struck, but if asked if it be a fair ball, he can, of course, say so; but he is not required to call fair balls.

THE SPECIAL RULES OF A BALL GROUND.—The Umpire, before calling "play," should see that the Captains of the contesting sides are mutually agreed upon what the rules of the ground are for the match. Thus, for instance, that a ball going over a fence shall give but one base, or that a ball taken on the fly from a tree, or the roof of a house, or the side of a fence, shall be regarded as a bound catch and only legitimate in the case of a foul ball; or that a ball passing the catcher, and being stopped by a fence too close to the home base, shall give one base, etc.

CALLING BALLS AND STRIKES.

CALLING BALLS ON PITCHERS.—This has hitherto been one of the most difficult duties of an Umpire; a study of these rules, however, will simplify matters considerably in this respect. The Umpire should first instruct himself in regard to the definition of unfair balls, and the following rules will give him the required information.

UNFAIRLY PITCHED BALLS.—A ball that strikes the ground in front of the home base is not a fair ball, as in the first place, by striking the ground, before reaching the batsman, it becomes a "bowled" ball, and secondly, because it is not pitched "over the home base and "fairly for the striker;" for unless it goes over the home base before touching the ground it is not "pitched" but "bowled" over, and unless so pitched it cannot be, "fairly for the striker.

A ball that is pitched on the side opposite to that the batsman habitually strikes from, is not a foul ball, because not pitched "for the striker."

A ball that is pitched so as to hit the striker—provided he is standing in his legitimate position, viz. with one foot on the line of the home base, and one foot from the base,—is not a fair one for the same reason. The striker should, however, stand far enough from the base to admit of the ball being pitched over it without its striking him.

Balls, too, which are pitched beyond the legitimate reach of the batsman, either in front of him or over his head are, for the same reason, not fair balls.

Certainly, all of the above balls are unfairly delivered, and can be legitimately regarded by the Umpire as balls to be called whenever pitched, provided due warning has been given the pitcher. Should the striker not stand in his position, as required by the 21st section of the rules, the Umpire is not required to call any of the above delivered balls as unfair balls.

WHAT THE RULE SAYS.—The rule—Section 6—states, that, "all balls, delivered by the pitcher, striking the ground before reaching the line of the home base; or pitched over the head of the batsman, or pitched to the side opposite to that which the batsman strikes from, shall be considered unfair balls;" and therefore all such balls must be called whenever pitched, after due warning has been given the pitcher. Thus, for instance, suppose the pitcher has sent in two or three balls within reach of the batsman and yet not what he wants, and the umpire warns him by saying "ball to the bat," and the next ball after such warning touches the ground in front of the home base; the umpire does not therefore call "one ball," because the pitcher has not thereby "repeatedly" failed to deliver fair balls but only once; but the next ball so pitched to the same striker, must be called "one ball," and the very next ball to that two balls. In case, however, two or three balls, out of *fair* reach of the bat, have been pitched, the Umpire after warning can call the very first ball touching the ground or sent overhead, etc., "one ball," and the very next after that "two balls," and this he not only may do but is obliged to do by the proper definition of the requirements of the rule. He only has option in calling balls in the case of those pitched "fairly for the striker," these he is to be the judge of in regard to their being fair or not; but all balls expressly stated to be unfair balls by the rules must be called as above directed.

CALLING STRIKES.—The umpire should be as strict in inflicting the penalty of the law on a batsman for failing to strike at fair balls for any special object, as he is in regard to the pitcher for unfair delivery. Hitherto impartial justice has not been the rule in this respect. When the striker is in his regular position, and fair balls are delivered to him—that is, balls within his legitimate reach, and " as near as possible over the home base," and " fairly for the striker "—the umpire, after warning him, should unhesitatingly call " strikes " on him. In judging of the action of the striker in this matter, and in inflicting the penalty of the law, the same rules apply as in the case of calling balls, viz., in interpreting the words " repeatedly " and " persists." Should the striker not stand on the base line, however, every ball—not expressly stated to be an unfair ball by the rule—passing at all near him, should be regarded as fair, and if he fails to strike at such ball " strikes " should be called on him. No law breaker himself can justly call for punishment on a similar offender.

The striker in calling for a " low ball " is not entitled to have one pitched to him lower than one foot from the base, as the pitcher could not well deliver balls lower without sending in balls striking the ground in front of the base.

No CAUSE JUSTIFIES UNFAIR DELIVERY.—The umpire should bear in mind that the words of the rule, in reference to a failure to deliver fair balls, are, " or for any cause." Therefore he should disregard the fact of the unfair pitching being unintentional, inasmuch as inability to deliver fair balls, whether arising from lack of skill in accuracy of delivery, or from too great a desire to pitch swiftly, is to be regarded as just cause for inflicting the penalty, as much so as wilfully unfair delivery would be. When, however, a ball is badly delivered from a palpable accident the umpire would be justified in letting it pass, but he should be assured of the true character of the error.

PITCHING FOR THE STRIKER.—The pitcher is required to deliver the ball " as near as possible over the centre of the home base " and " fairly for the striker." The correct interpretation is, that the pitcher must deliver to the batsman balls within the *legitimate* reach of his bat. What this legitimate reach is has been shown under the head of " Unfair Pitched Balls." Every experienced batsman has a peculiar and favorite style of hitting. Brinkerhoff—formerly of the Eagle club—could never hit a ball higher than a foot from the ground. P. O'Brien takes one very readily as high as his head. The generality of batsmen, however, require them about hip high. Now, this peculiarity of hitting is well known to all in the club a player belongs to, and can readily be ascertained, and when the umpire knows what ball the batsman is in the habit of striking at, he is then able to judge what a ball " fairly for the striker " should be. This done, he should not allow a player to suit his particular whim or fancy in the matter, but should consider every ball " fairly for the striker " that is pitched within reasonable distance of the point the batsman is in the habit of requiring a ball to be pitched to him. When a player is running his bases, and the period of the game is a critical one as regards the issue of the contest, we frequently find that a batsman who is in the habit of striking at balls hip high will call for a " low ball," in the hope that the pitcher, in his efforts to deliver a low ball, will pitch one likely to pass the catcher, in which case bases can be run by the player, that being the object of the striker in calling for " a low ball." This, of course, the striker has no right to do, and therefore the umpire cannot require a pitcher to send in such ball, unless the fact is well known that the batsman is in the habit of striking at low balls.

WARNING PLAYERS.—In regard to the warning required
to be given in cases of calling "balls" and "strikes,"
once being warned, for each striker, is sufficient. "Ball
to the bat" is all the warning necessary in regard to unfair delivery in pitching, and any simple word of caution
in reference to the penalty likely to be incurred, is all that
is requisite in the case of "strikes."

ON BALKING.

CALLING BALKS.—The point next in importance to that
of calling "balls" and "strikes" is that of judging of
balks. The rule—Section 7—states that : "The ball must
be pitched, not jerked or thrown, to the bat; and whenever
the pitcher moves with the apparent purpose or pretension
to deliver the ball, he shall so deliver it, and must have
neither foot in advance of the front line or off the ground
at the time of delivering the ball; and if he fails in either
of these particulars then it shall be declared a balk. The
ball shall be considered as jerked, in the meaning of the
rule, if the pitcher's arm touches his person when the arm
is swung forward to deliver the ball; and it shall be regarded as a throw if the arm be bent at the elbow, at an
angle from the body, or horizontally from the shoulder,
when it is swung forward to deliver the ball. A pitched
ball is one delivered with the arm straight, and swinging
perpendicularly, and free from the body."

It will be seen by the above rule that there are four distinct actions of the pitcher, each of which constitutes a
"balk," viz., *jerking* the ball; *throwing* the ball; *making any movement* with the apparent intent to deliver the
ball without delivering it, and having *either foot* outside of
the lines of his position, or off the ground, while in the
act of delivering the ball. Now the first thing to be done
is to define what a jerk or a throw is, as the other actions
are easily defined. The following are correct definitions :

WHAT A JERK IS.—A ball is "jerked"—in the meaning of the above rule—when an additional impetus is given the ball by any portion of the arm touching the side of the pitcher in the act of delivery. If the arm does not touch the side of the pitcher the ball is not jerked. Next as to a thrown ball :

WHAT A THROWN BALL IS.—The ordinary way of throwing a ball is over the shoulder, but a ball can also be thrown "underhand," that is, delivering it from the hand about knee-high or even lower. A ball, however, cannot be "thrown"—in the meaning of the rule—either by high or low delivery, unless the elbow is bent and a whip-like movement be given the arm in the act of delivery; consequently, if the arm be kept straight, and is swung in delivering the ball like the movement of a pendulum, no throw can be made. We next come to

THE MOVEMENT IN DELIVERING THE BALL.—Every pitcher has a peculiar style of delivering the ball. Some —like Faitoute of Eureka Club, for instance—have a series of movements in delivery; others simply have but a single swing of the arm in delivery. Now these movements are those which constitute the action alluded to in the rule, wherein it reads "*moves* with the apparent purpose or pretension to deliver the ball;" and from the period of the commencement of these preliminary movements, to the time of the delivering of the ball, is to be dated, the movement constituting a balk, if the ball is not delivered. For instance, suppose a pitcher takes three movements in delivering a ball—and none take less—viz. first, bending his body, then drawing his arm back, and lastly, swinging it forward to deliver the ball; if he fail to deliver the ball immediately after making either of these movements, a balk must be called, unasked. As a consequence, the pitcher making the fewest of these preliminary movements is the one most likely to deceive the player running the bases as to his intention to deliver the ball, without making a balk. The umpire should bear in mind that no warning is necessary prior to calling a "balk." We now come to the last point in judging of balks, and that is in reference to

HAVING BOTH FEET ON THE GROUND, WHEN ABOUT TO PITCH.—The rule in regard to this reads, "or off the ground at the time of delivering the ball." Now the sentence "time of delivering the ball" has been authoritatively defined by the Committee of Rules of the National Association, to mean, the swing of the arm, from the period of commencing to deliver, to the time the ball actually leaves the hand, and during this time both feet must be on the ground. From the above rules, it will be seen that whenever a pitcher jerks a ball, throws it, moves to deliver without delivering, or has either feet off the ground immediately preceding delivery, the umpire must call a balk unasked and without warning.

TAKING BASES ON BALKS.—The striker cannot take a base on a balk, for the reason that he is not considered "a player running the base," until he has struck a fair ball. Section 21, states that the striker "shall be considered the striker until he strikes a fair ball," but this only bears on the case of a player running home when two hands are out, or in reference to players vacating bases.

ON BASE PLAY.

IN JUDGING OF BASE PLAY.—From the position occupied by the umpire in judging of points of play around the bases, it is next to an impossibility for him to avoid making mistakes at times in his decisions; more latitude, therefore, should be allowed for errors of this kind than in any other instances occurring in a match. The following rules for judging of base play will be found advantageous in aiding the umpire in rendering correct decisions.

THE FIRST BASE.—The umpire must bear in mind that the "striker," running to the first base, is not out unless the ball is held on the base by the baseman *before* the striker touches it. If, at the same time, the striker is not out. It must be palpable that the ball was held on the base before the striker reached it, or he is not out. It should be remembered that the ball is to be held by the base-player with some part of his person touching the base at the same time. Touching the base with the *ball* in the player's hand, without some part of the player's person touching the base at the same time, does not put the striker out at first base. "Holding the ball on the base" means, having the ball in hand while standing on the base or touching it.

THE OTHER BASES.—This rule also applies to the other bases, in those cases wherein players are put out on them in a similar manner to that at first base, as in cases of being obliged to return to bases on fly catches or foul balls.

THE BASE BAG IS THE BASE.—The base bag is considered the base, not the post to which it is, or ought to be, fastened; therefore if "a player running the bases" touches the base bag with any part of his person, he cannot be put out, though the base bag be out of its place. The rule—Section 3—says, "The first, second and third bases shall be canvas bags."

TOUCHING PLAYERS.—When "judgment" is called on touching a player in running the bases, the Umpire should judge of the fact of the player's being touched more by the probability of the occurrence, from the proximity of the players to each other, rather than by the action of the base player in attempting to touch his adversary, as base players frequently are guilty of the trick of feigning to touch their opponents in order to deceive the umpire, when they are fully aware that he is either not within their reach, or has his foot on the base.

TOUCHING BASES.—If a player running the bases fails to touch any base as he runs round, he must return and touch it, and that, too, in the order of his running. Thus, for instance, if in running from first to home base he fails to touch the second base, he must return by the third base —touching it in returning—and go back to the second and touch it, and he can be put out by being touched by the ball before he reaches the second base in returning. Unless so touched, however, he is not out.

RUNNING BASES ON FOUL BALLS.—When a player is running his bases, and a foul ball is called, he must return to the base he left when the ball was struck,—or the one he left before it was struck, if he is running when it is struck—as the rule prohibits any base being made on a foul ball. In thus returning he should stand on the base until the ball is settled in the hands of the pitcher. Umpires should see that this is done, and should be particular in calling "foul" in a loud voice when a player is running his bases. In returning to a base, on a foul ball, he can be put out as at first base. The ball to be in play, —in the case of a foul ball—must have first been in the hands of the pitcher.

RUNNING BASES ON FLY BALLS.—When a fair fly ball has been caught, the player running his bases must return to his base he left when the ball was struck, as in the case of a foul ball. In the case of a foul ball, however, he has to wait on the base until the ball is settled in the hands of the pitcher; whereas in the case of a fair fly catch he can leave his base—after returning to it— the moment the ball is settled in the hands of the fielder catching it.

VACATING BASES.—If a player is on the first base when a *fair* ball is struck, he must immediately *vacate* it and run for his second; and if three players are on the bases when a fair ball is struck, each must promptly vacate the base he occupies and run for the next one—all, in such cases, being *forced* from their bases. Except under the above circumstances, however, they are not obliged to leave their bases. Thus, for instance: if there be no player on the first base, but one on the second or third, or both, and a fair ball be struck, neither of the players on the bases are obliged to leave them; and likewise, if there be a player on the first base and one on the third base when a fair ball is struck, it is only the player on the first base who is obliged to vacate his base. When players are thus obliged to vacate bases, they can be put out on the base they have to run to simply by the ball being held on the base before the player reaches it, there being no necessity to touch the player in order to put him out. In the case of players being on the first and third bases, too, when a fair ball is struck, if the ball be passed to the second base, all that is required is that it be held there before the player reaches it; but if the player on the third base is running home when a fair ball is struck, at the same time that the player on the first runs to the second, or if, having passed the second, he be running to the third, the player running home must be touched by the ball when off his base in order to be put out, and both he and the player running from second to third can return to the bases they last left, and can only be put out, in so returning, by being touched with the ball when off the base; but the player running from the first base, under the above circumstances, cannot return but to the second, as he was forced to leave his first base, but not his second. A very pretty point of play can be made when a player is forced from his first base. Thus, for instance : suppose a player is on the first base when a fair ground-ball is struck to short-field or the pitcher, and the player on the first, seeing that he is sure to be put out if he runs to the second base, decides to remain on the first and let the striker be first put out; if the ball in this instance, be sent to the first baseman, and he holds it on the base before the striker reaches it, the striker only is put out; but if, instead of receiving the ball while standing on the base, he receives it off the base, with no part of his person touching the base, and then, first touching the player standing on the base, puts his foot on the base before the striker reaches it, both players are out; inasmuch as, until the striker was put out, the player running the bases was forced to vacate the first base, and could be put out by being touched by the ball, even though he was standing on the base, for the reason that he was not legitimately entitled to stand there; the moment the striker was put out, however, that moment the player on the first ceased to be obliged to vacate his base, and had he been standing on the first base when the ball was first held on the base, and the baseman had *afterwards* touched him, he would not have been out, because the striker would, in that case, have been first out. The point of the play was in receiving the ball off the base in the first instance, then touching the player, and afterwards holding it on the base. In cases of sharp play like this, it is necessary that the umpire should have his wits about him to decide promptly and correctly.

RETURNING TO BASES.—Players running bases, when required to return to the base just left—as in the case of foul or fly balls—must return in the same order they make them. Thus : suppose a player is on the first base when a long ball is hit to the right or left field, and the ball looks as if it would strike fair, but the wind makes it fall foul, and the player, before " foul " can be called, has reached his third base, and is on his way home; the moment " foul " is called under these circumstances, he must return and *touch* the third and second bases, just the same as he did in running for the home base.

HOW BASES MUST BE MADE.—Bases must be made in the order of striking, and when a fair ball is struck and it is not caught on the fly, the first base, if occupied by a player, must be vacated, and likewise the second and third bases if they are occupied, and players may be put out under these circumstances in the same manner as the player running to first base. Thus, for instance, if there is a

player on the first base, when a ball is struck to the short
fielder, all the latter has to do is to pass it to the second
baseman, and if it be held on the base before the player
running from first to second base reaches it, the player in
question is out ; and if, after the ball is thus held, it be
passed quickly to the first base, and held there before the
player reaches it who is running to that base, of course the
latter is out also, this passing of the ball in time thus constituting a "double play." Should three players be on their
bases when a fair ball is struck to the short-stop, all the
fielders have to do is, first, to pass the ball to the catcher at home base, he to the third baseman, and the latter
to the second baseman, and if the ball he held on the base
in each instance before the player running the bases reaches the base he is obliged to run for, all three are out. But
if there be a player on the second base and one on the
third, and none on the first, and a fair ball be struck to the
short-field and not caught on the fly, neither of the players
are obliged to vacate their bases ; in this case, the ball
must be passed to first base in order to put the batsman
out. Under no other circumstances then, as above enumerated are players forced to vacate their bases.

OBSTRUCTING PLAYERS AND FIELDERS.—In reference to
the rule which declares any player out if he "intentionally" obstructs a fielder in catching or stopping a ball,
and which gives a player his base if a fielder or base player "intentionally" prevents him from making it, the
Umpire, before he gives his decision, must be *sure*, in the
first instance, that the player does not wilfully get in the
way of the fielder or base player, and secondly that the
latter does not wilfully prevent his adversary from making
his base. He should not, of course, hesitate in giving his
decision, but when he does give it he should not be in
doubt on the subject, but feel satisfied that the obstruction
was "intentional." The word "intentional" in the rule,
refers to actions *which could have been avoided.* For in-

stance, it is required by the rules that a player running the bases should avoid, if possible, running in the way of a fielder while the latter is trying to catch or stop the ball, and it is also incumbent upon the fielder or base player to allow his adversary free access to the base he is running for. When there is any doubt on the subject, the Umpire should decide in favor of the party obstructed. Thus, if a fielder happens to be standing on the line of a base to catch a falling ball, the player, running the bases, has no right to run up against him because he happens to be between him and the base he is running to, for he could run a few feet to one side without being prevented by the fielder from reaching his base by the latter's effort to catch the ball. But this running out of the line of his base must only be done when it is not to avoid the ball in the hands of a fielder. In regard also to a base-player taking a ball from a fielder, the former has no right to stand between the player and the base he is running to, when the ball could be equally well taken by standing out of the way of his adversary. In such instances as these the obstruction should be regarded as intentional, in the spirit of the law, from the fact that it could have been avoided, though perhaps the obstruction was not actually intended.

RUNNING OUT OF THE LINE OF THE BASES.—The umpire should bear in mind that unless the player running the bases runs out of the line of the bases to *avoid* the ball in the hands of a fielder, he is not to be given out. When a long hit is made and the striker makes a home run he invariably runs out of the line of his bases, but he is not therefore liable to be put out for doing it. It is only when he does it to avoid the ball that the penalty is to be inflicted.

ON POINTS OF PLAY NOT SEEN.—The umpire has no right to take the testimony of players or spectators, in regard to any play he has not seen, nor has he a right to decide on any point of play which he has not himself witnessed. He alone is the judge of the play, and if he has not seen a player touched with the ball or a ball caught, he has no right to decide the player, touched or caught, out. There are cases when the testimony of hundreds can be accepted, as in the instance of a foul ball catch outside the circle of spectators, or a fly catch taken close to the ground in the outer field near the circle of spectators, when the testimony of those in the vicinity of the catch may be fully relied on. But unless such overwhelming proof be afforded, the umpire should only decide on points of play actually seen by himself.

How THE STRIKER CAN BE PUT OUT.—The striker can be put out on a foul ball caught either on the fly or bound, and on a fair ball, caught on the fly, and by the ball being held on the first base before he reaches it. He can also be put out by being touched by the ball, after he has struck a fair ball and before he reaches his first base.

WHAT CONSTITUTES A FOUL BALL.—A ball, to be foul, must strike the ground, the person of a player, or any other object *behind* the line of the bases, or it is not a foul ball. If it strikes the *line* of the bases it is a *fair* ball; it must strike behind the line of the bases to be foul. Suppose, for instance, the foul ball touches the back part of the home base, it becomes a foul ball from the fact that it thereby strikes behind the " range " of the home base, the " range "—or line of the base—starting from the centre of the base. Again—suppose the ball is struck to left or right fields in such a manner that, if not stopped or caught by a fielder, it would strike the ground fair, but that, by the action of the fielder, who is standing within the foul ball line, it touches his hands within and rebounds outside the foul ball line, the umpire must consider it a *fair* ball. Suppose, also, that a ball similarly hit to the right or left fields, touches the branch of a tree or the roof of a house, which object is within the line of the bases, and the ball glances off and falls to the ground, outside those lines, it is also to be considered a fair ball, these objects being considered just the same as the ground in such cases.

SCORING RUNS.—No run can be legitimately recorded until the player running home *touches the home base*, and not then, if two hands are out when he is running home: and the batsman be caught out, either on a fair or foul ball, or be touched between home and first base. Should the batsman make his first base, and be immediately put out in running to either of the other bases, then the player running home, when two hands are out, can score his run; but not then, even, unless he touches the base before the player running the bases is put out, for the moment the player is put out under such circumstances the innings terminates, and no run can then be legitimately scored. The umpire should watch the ball, and the action of the player touching the home base, as closely as possible under these circumstances.

WHEN THE BALL IS DEAD.

NO PLAYER CAN BE PUT OUT ON A DEAD BALL.—There are several positions of play in the game when the ball is what is technically termed "dead," and not in play, and when this is the case no player can be put out by being touched or caught. For instance, the ball is "dead" until it is settled in the hands of the pitcher when he is within the lines of his position, after being stopped in any way by the crowd of spectators, or by any one not engaged in the game. Again, it is "dead," until settled in the hands of the pitcher, after it has been struck foul, (except as far as a fly or bound catch is concerned,) no player running the bases on a foul ball being liable to be put out until after the ball has been held by the pitcher. It is also "dead," in regard to the striker, when a "balk" or a "ball" is called, until it is again settled in the hands of the pitcher. Let us illustrate these cases of dead balls.

WHAT THE RULE SAYS.—Section 10 (new section) says : " Any ball delivered by the pitcher on which a balk or a ball has been called, shall be considered *dead* and not in play, until it has been settled in the hands of the pitcher, while he stands within the lines of his position, and no such ball, if hit, shall put the striker out."

BALLS STOPPED BY SPECTATORS.—When a fair ball is hit, or when a ball is thrown from one player to another, the umpire should watch the ball and see that it is neither stopped by the crowd nor handled by any one not engaged in the game, for in either case the ball must first be settled in the hands of the pitcher before it is again in play, and that, too, while he is standing within the lines of his position. Suppose, for instance, the striker hits a ball to the third baseman, and he throws it wildly to the first base, and it goes by the base player and is stopped by the crowd, the ball cannot be fielded by the fielder who goes after it, to the baseman, or to any other fielder, to put the player running his bases out, until it has first been settled in the hands of the pitcher, and held by him while standing within the lines of his position.

A BALKED BALL.—Should the pitcher move his foot in delivery—thereby making a "balk"—and the Umpire call a "balk" until the ball is returned to the pitcher, no player can be put out on it, either on three strikes or by being caught on the fly, or on a foul fly or bound catch, the ball being made "dead" by the balk. Should the balk made, too, be as above or one from making a false movement, the ball is not in play until the player running his bases has made the base he had to make, reasonable time being allowed for his making it. Should the striker hit the balked ball fair, he cannot take his base on it, as the balked ball is not a "fair" ball, and until the striker hits a fair ball or has a base given him on three balls, he cannot run to his base.

A FOUL BALL.—In the case of a foul ball, struck when a player is running his bases, the player can return to his base even if the baseman has the ball in hand on the base the player has to return to, unless the ball has been in the pitcher's hands first. For instance, suppose a player on the third base, or running home, when a foul ball is struck to left field, and the ball be thrown in by the fielder to the third baseman, and the latter touch the player while he is off the base instead of first sending the ball to the pitcher, the player, of course, is *not out*. The point of play, in this case, is, for the pitcher to run to the third base and receive the ball from the fielder, and if he holds it before the player can get back to the base—the pitcher touching the base while the ball is in hand—the player is out, and that, too, without being touched.

ON THREE STRIKES.—Should a "balk" be called by the umpire—say on account of the pitcher moving his foot, for instance—and the striker strike at the ball for the third time, and miss it, and it be caught on the bound by the catcher, the striker is *not out*, as the ball, the moment the "balk" was called, was made "dead," and not in play. Again, should the umpire call a "ball," and the striker strike at it, and hit it fair, and it be caught on the fly, or sent to first base and there held, the striker is *not out*, as the moment the "ball" was called, the ball ceased to be in play. Again, too, in the case of a fly or foul "tip," the same result follows if the umpire call a "balk" or a "ball." In fact, no player can be put out, in such case, until after the ball has been returned to and held by the pitcher, while in his position, after the "balk" has been made or the "ball" called; the ball, under such circumstances, being considered as "dead," and not in play, just as it is in the case of a foul ball when a player is running his bases, no player running the bases being liable to be put out until the pitcher has first held the ball after "foul" has been called.

PLAYING INTO THE DARK.

PLAYING GAMES INTO THE DARK.—There is no more difficult, and certainly no more unpleasant, duty of an Um-

pire than that of deciding when a game shall be called,
when it has been played until darkness has set in. In
the first place there is no rule that could be adopted which
would obviate the difficulty, except, perhaps, that of requiring a game to be commenced at noon, and therefore the
discretionary power of calling a game is necessarily left in
the hands of the umpire. Secondly, in close contests between rival clubs, when the issue of the match is important, experience has shown that no Club is free from the
tendency to allow their desire to win, to overcome their
innate love of fair play under such circumstances; and
hence we find that in just such contests, when the last innings of the game is being played after sunset, the party
who lead the score on the last even innings. if in the field,
are far too apt to be seized with a fit of short sightedness,
and if at the bat either be over particular in the character of the balls they want pitched to them, or, if two hands
are out, and there is no chance of closing the innings before it really becomes too dark to play, they have a great
tendency to imagine unfair balls just the thing to suit
them; the result being that they wilfully strike out.
Now the umpire, being expressly declared the sole judge
of fair and unfair play in the game, as such a judge possesses an arbitrary power in deciding on disputed points,
which nothing but the express wording of any special law
can overrule; and hence, under such circumstances in a
match as occur when wilfully unfair play is shown by
either party, either purposely to delay a game, or to has-
ten its close, as the interests of either of the contesting
clubs may require, the umpire should avail himself of this
arbitrary power to nullify the unfair play as much as possible; and to assist him in his decisions in this respect,
we give below a few rules which experience has shown to
be necessary to be followed in order to put a stop to the
unmanly and discreditable style of play known as " playing a game into the dark. First we give

WHAT THE RULE SAYS.—Section 15 says, " If three

balls are struck at and missed, and the last is caught, either before touching the ground or upon the first bound, provided the balls struck at are not those on which balls or balks have been called, or not those struck at for the purpose of wilfully striking out," the striker is out.

FIRST.—If the party at the bat lead the score on the last even innings played, and are just finishing the first part of the following innings, and it is evident that there is no time to play the inning out; or if the game is in that position when it is manifestly to their advantage to throw it back to the even innings played, and in order to do so it becomes necessary for their players to get out as soon as they can—say, for instance, by striking out—the umpire, when he sees a batsman strike at a ball either too far off, too high, or too low for him to hit, should refuse to call strikes on him, and this he can legally do, for unless a ball be fairly delivered to the bat, it is not a ball to call strikes on. The rule just quoted, however, gives him full power in the premises.

SECOND.—If the party in the field are so situated in regard to the issue of the contest as to make it a "point of play," for them to prolong the innings as much as possible, or to have the game "called" on the last even innings played, and the Umpire perceives that they do not field balls which ought to be fielded, or that their pitcher is purposely delivering unfair balls in order to delay the game until it is clearly too dark to play, he may consider every ball within possible reach of the bat as a fair ball, and justly call strikes on the batsman when he strikes at such balls and fails to hit them.

THIRD.—When a game is in the position above described, and the fielders contend that they cannot see the ball, if the Umpire finds that it is light enough for him to distinctly follow the ball with his eye, from the bat to the field, he should allow the game to proceed; but the moment he cannot do so, he should call the game without regard to the position the respective contestants are placed in. He alone must judge of the matter, and he should not take testimony from either side as to its being too dark or otherwise.

No Law of the Game can be Ignored.—If the Umpire perceives, during the progress of a match, that any special rule of the game is being mutually ignored by the contesting clubs, he should at once retire from the field, and proclaim the game as *null* and *void;* for rule 38 states that " Any match game played by any club, in contravention of the rules adopted by this Association, shall be considered null and void, and shall not be counted in the list of match games won or lost." Should rain or any sufficient cause require a postponement of a match, the same can be " put off by mutual consent of the parties about engaging in a game."

OTHER DUTIES.

No Game to be Commenced in the Rain.—Rule 38 expressly prohibits a match game from being commenced in the rain. Should it rain at the the time appointed to commence play in a match, the contesting clubs can mutually agree to postpone the game to some other day.

When Play can be Suspended.—The power to " call " a game at any time—that is, to suspend play entirely—is left in the hands of the umpire. If from any just cause a game cannot be concluded, it shall be decided by the last even innings played—provided five innings have been played—and the party having the greatest number of runs shall be declared the winner. It will be seen by section 33 of the rules that it is discretionary with the Umpire when a game shall terminate, of course providing that there is any legitimate cause of interruption : such as a fall of rain, the interference of a crowd of spectators, or the approach of darkness. The law says, " if the game cannot be concluded," this sentence of course limiting the discretionary power of the Umpire to a legitimate cause for closing the game, such for instance as rain or darkness, &c.

REVERSING DECISIONS.—When once a decision has been made it should never be reversed, unless the error is immediately palpable to the Umpire. But if arising from any explanation made by either of the contesting parties, no reversal should follow. Of course in a case where the Umpire makes an illegal decision, and his error in ruling is promptly made apparent, he will be justified in correcting himself in the matter; but, as a general thing, hold to the decision made. No error in ruling on a disputed point should be corrected, or any decision reversed, after the ball has been delivered fairly to the batsman after the occurrence of the point of play in dispute.

DISMISSING TRANSGRESSORS.—The Umpire has the power to order the dismissal of any player from a nine in a match, if he ascertains that any one of the players is either interested in any *bet* made upon the result, or that he is a *member of another club*, or that he has *not* been a member of the club he plays with for the required thirty days immediately prior to the game he plays in, or if he is *paid for his services as a player* in the game he takes part in.

WHO CAN ACT AS UMPIRE.—No one can act as umpire in a match, played by clubs belonging to the National Association, unless he is a member of a club belonging to and governed by the rules thereof.

NAMING THE WINNING CLUB.—The umpire, before leaving the ground, must record the name of the winning club in the score books of both the contesting clubs, over his own signature. Until such record is made no club can claim the ball won in a match.

GENERAL HINTS TO UMPIRES.

Never *hesitate* in giving a decision if you can possibly avoid it. There are, of course, times when the movements of the players are so rapid, and appeals are made on two or three points at once, where the Umpire is very likely to become confused. When this occurs, never give a man out on a doubt. The players, on the " in " side, may be regarded as prisoners at the bar are in jury trials, and as such are to be given all the benefit of a doubt, and must be proved guilty before being punished. In the game a player must be plainly out, or he should be given in.

No one should accept the position of Umpire who is not conversant with the amended rules of the game, for he is not competent to act unless he is. Those who have leisure time should familiarize themselves in the position by acting in practice games. Umpiring, like playing, requires practice.

Those who act this season should post themselves up in the amendments. For the benefit of Umpires we give the principal amendments in brief below.

First.—The pitcher's line is reduced from twelve to six feet.

Second.—Balls bounding to the bat, going over the batsman's head, or to the side he does not strike from, are " unfair " balls and *must* be called after warning.

Third.—A *jerked* ball is one delivered by touching the side of the body with the arm. A *thrown* ball is one sent in with the elbow bent. A *pitched* ball can only be sent in with a straight arm, swinging perpendicular.

Fourth.—The striker is such only until he has hit a fair ball, then he becomes " a player running the bases."

Fifth.—A *balked* or *called* ball is *dead*, and no player can be put out on it. Neither can the striker make a base on a balked ball or on a called ball, unless, in the latter case it be the third ball called.

Sixth.—No batsman can be put out on three strikes if the third ball he strikes at be a *balked or called* ball. And no strike at such a ball, is to be counted; and likewise no strike made purposely to strike out.

Seventh.—The striker must have one foot on the line of his position when he hits the ball, and cannot take a step either backward or forward when striking at the ball.

Eighth.—When a ball is stopped by the crowd of spectators in any way, it becomes *dead*, and is not in play again until the pitcher has held it while standing within the lines of his position.

Ninth.—No player running home when two hands are out, can score his run if the batsman be put out before making his 1st base.

Tenth.—The Umpire must not only call all foul balls, but also call out how and by whom a player is put out. Thus if the striker be put out at first base he must call out, " Striker out at first base."

Eleventh.—All persons who play ball for money are now called " professional players," and as such cannot play in any match played by any Association club; and any Umpire learning that such a player is in a nine in a match in which he is acting must at once call " time," insist upon the professional being removed from the nine, or resign his position as Umpire, thereby making the game " null and void."

The above are the only amendments affecting the RULES OF PLAY, in which the Umpire is concerned   Allow no players to stand or sit by you when Umpiring for your attention will thereby be distracted from the game.

When you take your position, resolve in your mind what rule you will observe in regard to calling balls, and when you have fixed upon a special rule adhere to it through the game.   Unless you do this your decisions will vary so much in the course of a game as to bear the appearance of being partial, when you really have acted impartially.

Never let a partisan crowd intimidate you.   The prominent trait of a good Umpire is *moral courage,* and once let an assemblage of spectators see that you are fearless in discharging the duties of your position and you will find that the respectable portion are with you, and the opinion of those only should you respect.

If you should happen to be Umpire where the " roughs " —low blackguards who scorn an honest living—are in the ascendancy, treat their remarks with contemptuous silence, as if they were so many yelping curs. Never reply to taunts, but as long as the players are satisfied, keep to your post. But should either of the contesting nines be guilty of such conduct, resign your position at once. This would end the game, for no true ball player would act as umpire, after another had resigned under such circumstances.

If you think yourself competent to act, and the clubs asking you are respectable organizations, never hesitate to act at once, for it is a compliment to you to be selected. The position of Umpire is the most honorable one a ball player can occupy, and any man should feel proud of excelling in it or of being considered a first rate Umpire.

If a player should, in the excitement of a game, dispute your decision in any way, do not let the occurrence prejudice you to the extent of giving a decision against him, when he happens to be the defendant in the case of appeal. Such a petty revenge is unworthy of a ball player.

Keep cool ; watch the ball all the time, and decide by the first impression of the play, and you cannot go far wrong.

HOW TO SCORE IN BASE BALL.

To score a game of base ball is a simple thing to do, provided the batting only be recorded; but if the particulars of the fielding be required, then more work is necessary. Below will be found the regular system of scoring endorsed by the National Association, and practiced by all the best scorers in the country.

TO SCORE THE BATTING.

When the players take their positions in the field, and the game commences, all the scorer has to do to record the particulars of the batting, is, the moment a run is secured,

to put down a dot (.) in the corner of the square opposite
the name of the batsman making the run ; and when an
out is made all he has to do is to mark down the figure 1,
for the first out, 2 for the second out, and 3 for the third.
By way of checking the score, he can also record each run
at the end of the score of each batsman, so that the batsman's total score at the end of each innings can be seen at
a glance.

When the innings terminate, add up the total dots or
runs recorded, and mark the figure underneath the column
of the inning, and underneath this figure record the grand
total at the close of each innings. Thus suppose 3 runs
are scored in the 1st inning, and 2 in the 2d and 3 in the
3d, under the total figure of the 2d innings you mark down
5 and under the total figure of the 3d innings you mark
down the figure 8; by this means you can tell at a glance
what the total score of a player or of an innings is at any
time during the game. The above rule is simply the method
of scoring the runs and outs made, without the particulars
of the fielding.

TO SCORE THE FIELDING

To record the manner in which each player is out requires a system of abbreviations, and the following is the
one now in general use, and endorsed by the National
Association. The abbreviations used are very simple and
are easily remembered. For instance A, B and C stand
for the 1st, 2d and 3d bases, and for recording everything
else, the first or last letter of the word to be abbreviated, is
used. Thus for the word " fly," the letter F is used ;
for the word " bound," the letter D is used, because B,
the first letter of the word is used to designate the 2d
base. For the word " foul," L is used because F
represents " fly." Now these are the fundamental abbreviations used to record the majority of outs in a match, and
by way of illustration we will proceed to score a game,
using simply the above abbreviations.

A GAME SCORED.

In recording the fielding score of a game, it is first necessary that each batsman and fielder's name be designated by a figure, and they are numbered from one to nine, in the order in which they strike. The accompanying diagram will illustrate this order, and an explanation of the abbreviations used in it will be found in the account of the game which follows. The score recorded is that of the Union Club in their match with the Eckfords, June 6th, 1866.

(SEE TABLE ON NEXT PAGE.)

Now, this table is a complete record of the batting of the Unions and the fielding of the Eckfords in the above match, and the explanation of the abbreviations used are as follows :

Smith was the first striker, and went out on three strikes, which is recorded by the figure " 1 " for the first out, and the letter K to indicate how put out, K being the last letter of the word " struck." The letter K is used in this instance as being easier to remember in connection with the word struck than S, the first letter, would be.

Abrams was second striker and second out, and was put out at first base by Klein, and this is recorded by the figure " 2 " for second out, and the figure " 4 " for Klein —he being 4th on the list of the Eckford nine—with the letter A for 1st base. Birdsall then scored a run, and this is recorded by a dot in the corner of the square. Martin was on his 3d base, when Pabor went out on a tip-bound, and this is recorded first by placing the small figure and letter " 3d " in the corner of Martin's square, and then in Pabor's the figure " 3 " for 3d out, and the small figure " 5 " for Beach's name, and the letters TD for tip bound, the total score of the innings being one run, which is recorded at the bottom of the column of the first innings.

Ketchum was the first striker in the 2d innings, and he was caught on the fly by Grum, recorded thus, " 1 F."

Batsmen.	1	2	3	4	5	6	7	8	9	Fielders.
1 Smith, 1st B.	k 1	5 L F 3								1 Grum, C. F.
2 Abrams, 3d B.	4 A 2		3d		1 F 1					2 Brown, 2d B.
3 Birdsall, C.		3d		2-4 A 1	8-2 B 2			4 A 2		3 Zettlein, P.
4 Martin, 2d B.	3d		8-2 L 2		2-4 A 3			3d		4 Klein, 1st B.
5 Pabor, P.	5 T 1 3		5 L 1 5 L F 2			2-4 A 1	4 2	F 3 L F 3		5 Beach, C.
6 Ketchum, C. F.		1 F 1		8-4 A 2		2 1 2	7-5 H 3		6-4 A 1	6 Mills, 3d B.
7 Akin, L. F.		.	5 L F 3			5 L F 3		5 L F 1	8 F 2	7 Swandell, R. F.
8 Bassford, R. F.		15-9 C 2			.		2-4 A 1	.	7 F 3	8 McDonald, S. S.
9 Hannegan, S. S.	.	.						.		9 Ryan, L. F.
Totl.	1	2	0	0	3	0	5	4	0	
Grand Total,	3	8	3	0	3	11	15	15		

Akin then made a run—recorded with a dot ; Bassford was put out at 3d base by Beach and Mills, recorded by the figures 5 for Beach, (who threw the ball,) and 6 for Mills, (who touched the player). Hannegan then made a run—another dot—and Smith was caught out on a foul fly by Beach, recorded by the figure 5 (for Beach) and letters L F for foul fly. Two runs were scored in this innings, and 2 is the figure recorded at the foot of the column, the figure 3 being placed underneath to indicate the grand total at the close of the 2d innings.

It is scarcely necessary to further describe the score, as by this time the reader will have learnt how to follow it out himself. This score includes nearly all the abbreviations used in a game; but sometimes more are used, and the following list, with their definitions will be found complete for recording every particular of the game :

A for first base.	D for catch on the bound.
B for second base.	L for foul balls.
C for third base.	T for tips.
H for home base.	K for struck out.
F for catch on the fly.	R for run out between bases.

Double letters—H R, or h r, for home runs.

L F for foul ball on the fly.
L D for foul ball on the bound
T F for tip on the fly.
T D for tip on the bound.

• for a run; 1st, 2d or 3d for left on bases, according to the base.

" Foul fly " or " foul bound " catches are those made from high balls in the air. " Tip fly " or " tip bound " catches are those made from foul balls sharp from the bat to the catcher.

SCORING.

HINTS TO SCORERS.

PASSED BALLS are those that are missed or muffed by the catcher, thereby admitting of the player running a base; none but those on which bases are run are counted as passed balls.

HOME RUNS are made when the batsman goes the round of the bases on his hit and reaches home before being touched with the ball. In the first place, however, no home run can be fairly scored if the player running home is obliged to stop on any of the three bases to avoid being put out. Of course, it does not follow in all cases that, because he does not stop on the bases in running round, that he thereby makes a home run. In recording home runs, only score runs as home runs which are made from hits to the outer field, out of the reach of the fielders, on which the home base is made by the striker before the ball is returned to the catcher, or passes the home base. These are what is called clean home runs, and are the only runs of the kind meriting a special record. Home runs made from errors in the field, in the way of gross failures to stop a ball or from wild throws, should not be counted as such.

STRIKING OUT, is when a batsman strikes three times at a ball, and failing to hit it is either caught out by the catcher, or put out at the first base. In both cases it is recorded as "struck out;" and not as being out from the catch or at the base.

FLY CATCHES.—Under this head every fly catch is recorded, whether foul or fair.

FOUL BALLS.—Fly or bound catches, either from foul balls or "tips," are all included under the head of "foul balls."

MISSED CATCHES.—Charge a catch as missed, if the ball touches the fielder's hands and he fails to hold it.

LEFT ON BASES.—The number of times a player is left

on bases, should be recorded, as it frequently happens that a good hit fails to be rewarded with a run, from the fault of the striker following the one making the hit.

RUN OUT.—When a player is put out between the bases, from being touched, he is charged with being "run out," and the credit of the fielding goes to the player touching him.

RUNS NOT TO BE SCORED.—No player running home at the time the ball is struck, when two hands are out, can score his run if the batsman be put out before reaching the first base. Neither is a player running home, when two hands are out, entitled to score his run unless he touches the base before the third hand is out.

SCORING IN PRIZE GAMES.—All prizes are awarded to those making the most runs and fewest outs, in the case of prizes given for the best batting; and for the most fly catches in fielding. In prize games it is necessary that the scorer be careful in recording the play of the batsman. For instance he should put down the number of bases he makes on his hit, whether he only makes his first base or his second or third on the strike ; and also the base he is left on, for in a tie score of runs and outs between two contestants the number of bases on hits, and times left on bases would have to be taken into consideration. The true test of merit in batting is the number of bases made by the hit against good fielding, not, of course, taking in loose play in the field, such as gross failures to stop balls or wild throws.

ABBREVIATIONS FOR RECORDING THE FIELDING.

ERRORS of play in the field as well as good points made, should be recorded, and our plan of doing this is as follows.

WILD THROWING.—For a wild throw we simply mark down a line with a dot in the centre, the dot being placed above or below the line as the throw is over head or on the ground. Thus _____•_____ or thus ‾‾‾•‾‾‾ Of course we place the figure of the player's name who makes the throw over the line indicating the throw.

MISSED CATCHES.—A missed catch we record by a simple circle for a fly ball missed thus, $\bigcirc$ ' or a circle with a dot in the centre for a bound ball missed, thus, $\odot$, placing the figure of the player's name over it.

MUFFED BALL.—For a badly muffed ball we use a large dot ● ; for a slight muff a small one, thus ● placing the figure of the player's name over it.

BASES MADE.—For every base made we make a mark in the upper corner of the square. Thus if one base be made by the hit we record it, thus, ┼; if two bases, thus, ═╪═ ; if three bases, thus, ╪ and if a home run, thus, ╪, adding "H. R." over the dot of the run in the latter instance.

WHERE THE BALL IS HIT.—To record where the ball is hit and its character, whether a high ball, a bounding ball or a "grounder," we simply add dots to the base marks, thus. If a "grounder," is hit to centre field on which two bases are made we mark it thus ╪ ; if the hit was to the right field, and a high ball, we should record it thus, ╪ ; if a bounding ball to the left field, we should simply make the mark thus, ╪ If the ball was hit to 1st base we place the dot on the end of the mark, thus, ┼ ; if to 3d base thus ; if to 2d base, thus, . A poor hit—say a high ball dropping in the in field—we mark, thus, ; and a poor hit on the ground, thus,

PASSED BALLS.—These are simply recorded by the letter P. Passed balls are those muffed by the catcher, and on which bases are made. If the base is not made, the error is not marked down.

OVER-PITCHED BALLS.—An over-pitched ball is marked thus, , with the figure of the pitcher's name over it.

GOOD FIELDING.—A specially good play we record thus : placing the figure of the player's name over it.

DOUBLE PLAYS.—A double play is recorded by a brace, thus, connecting the two squares in which the outs are recorded.

NAMING PLAYERS WHO ASSIST.—When a player is put out on the bases—say, at first base—by a throw of a fielder, we record it, thus : the base player's figure being 4, and the fielder's, 2

MISSED FOUL BALLS.—When foul balls are missed we record them as follows : a foul fly, thus, ; a foul bound thus, ; a fly tip, thus, ; a tip bound thus,

CHANGES OF POSITION.—When the positions of players are changed, such as the pitcher going to the field and the fielder to pitch, we record it at the top of the column, as follows: Suppose the left-fielder should be the third striker on the list, and the pitcher the eighth, and they should change places in the third innings, we place the following marks at the top of the column of the third inning, viz. 3 P. 8 L, which means that No. 3 went in to pitch, and No. 8 to left-field.

STRIKING TWICE.—When a batsman has two or more turns at the bat we make two or more squares in the column of the innings, and in recording the play the first figures should be made close to the line so as to allow for another square.

HOW RUNS ARE MADE.—When a batsman gets home, we record how he made his run, viz., by placing a mark over the dot which marks the run, which will indicate how he got home. Thus if he gets home on a passed ball, we place P over the dot of the run. If he is sent home by the striker, we place the figure of the striker's name over the dot. If he steal home on the catcher or pitcher, we place the letters " St." indicating " Stolen " over the dot. If on a wild throw, the line thus,＿＿●＿ ; and so on.

RUNNING OUT.—When a player makes his base after being nearly run out we record it by the letters " n. r. o."

THREE MEN ON BASES.—When three men on the bases, we draw a line connecting the three squares with the figure 3 attached to it drawing the line on the left of the column line.

SPECIAL HITS.—Sometimes the batsman hits a fine ball deserving two or more bases, but from good fielding, a fear of consequences, or laziness, takes only one base for it; in such cases we add a cross to the mark indicating the one base made, thus, $\not\uparrow$

DIFFICULT CATCHES.—Sometimes balls are missed being caught, which, though misses in one sense, are not errors of play or muffed catches, in which cases we not only record it as a missed catch, thus, ◯ , but make a cross over it, thus, ⊗ to show that the effort to catch it redeemed the failure to hold it.

By means of the above abbreviations the rapid movements of the player can be instantly recorded, and a detailed report of a game made up from the figures and marks placed in a very small space.

THE MODEL BASE BALL PLAYER.

THIS is an individual not often seen on a ball ground, but he nevertheless exists ; and as a description of his characteristics will prove advantageous, we give a pen photogram of him, in the hope that his example will be followed on all occasions, for if it were, an end would at once be put to many actions which now give rise to unpleasantness on our ball grounds.

HIS MORAL ATTRIBUTES.

The principal rule of action of our model base ball player is, to comport himself like a gentleman on all occasions, but especially on match days, and in so doing he abstains from *profanity* and its twin and vile brother obscenity, leaving these vices to be alone cultivated by graduates of our penitentiaries

He always has his temper under control, and takes everything good humoredly, or if angered at all, makes an effort and keeps silent.

He never censures errors of play made by a brother member or an opponent, as he is well aware that faultfinding not only leads to no improvement in the play of the

one who blunders, but on the contrary is calculated to
have the very reverse effect.

He was never known to dispute the decision of an Umpire, for knowing the peculiar position an Umpire is
placed in, he is careful never to wound his feelings
by implying that his judgment is weak, his partiality apparent, or his integrity of character doubtful, one or other
of these imputations being made whenever that official's
decision is disputed by a player. Moreover, he is never
guilty of questioning the decision of the Umpire by his
actions, which, in many instances, are as expressive in this
respect as words; but, when judgment has been rendered,
he silently acquiesces in the decision, whatever it may be.

He never takes an ungenerous advantage of his opponents, but acts towards them as he would wish them to
act towards himself. Regarding the game as a healthful
exercise, and a manly and exciting recreation, he plays it
solely for the pleasure it affords him, and if victory crowns
his efforts in a contest, well and good; but should defeat
ensue he is equally ready to applaud the success obtained
by his opponents; and by such action he robs defeat of
half its sting, and greatly adds to the pleasure the game
has afforded both himself and his adversaries.

He never permits himself to be pecuniarily interested in
a match, for knowing the injurious tendency of such a
course of action to the best interests of the game, he
values its welfare too much to make money an object in
view in playing ball.

He is ever prompt in his engagements, is punctually in
attendance on the field on match days; readily obeys the
commands of the presiding officer of the day; plays the
game throughout, whether winning or losing, to the best
of his ability, and retires from the field apparently content
with the result whatever it may be.

He abides by every rule of the game, as long as it is
legally in force; if it should not meet with his approval he
awaits the proper time to have it erased from the statute

books; but he never ignores its existence as long as it is legally a rule of the game.

The physical qualifications of our model player are as follows: To be able to throw a ball with accuracy of aim a dozen or a hundred yards.

To be fearless in facing and stopping a swiftly batted or thrown ball.

To be able to catch a ball either on the "fly," or bound, either within an inch or two of the ground, or eight or ten feet from it, with either the right or left hand or both.

To be able to run swiftly, and to check himself suddenly, and to pick up a ball while running.

To be able to hit a swiftly pitched ball or a "slow twister" with equal skill, and also to command his bat so as to hit the ball either within six inches of the ground or as high as his shoulder, and either towards the right, centre or left fields, as occasion may require.

To be able to occupy any position on the field creditably, but to excel in one position only. To be familiar, practically and theoretically, with every rule of the game and "point" of play.

To conclude our description of a model base ball player, we have to say, that his conduct is as much marked by courtesy of demeanor and liberality of action as it is by excellence in a practical exemplification of the beauties of the game ; and his highest aim is to characterize every contest in which he may be engaged, with conduct that will mark it as much as a trial as to which party excels in the moral attributes of the game, as it is one that decides any question of physical superiority.

HOW TO ORGANIZE A CLUB.

IN organizing a club, it should be remembered that the Constitution of the National Association requires each Club entering the Association to be composed of not less than eighteen active members, that is, men who actively engage in play on practice days, and who take part in match games.

The corps of officers requisite, consists of a President, Secretary and Treasurer. A Club can, of course, add a Vice-President and Corresponding Secretary.

Honorary members of Clubs can also act as active members, in being appointed delegates and representatives; the privilege of voting at club meetings, however, is denied them.

It is desirable to secure the services of one or two men in a Club who will take as much interest in its welfare as if it was a pet stock company, yielding them large pecuniary returns. Without such supporters, no club will flourish long as a general thing.

Don't elect bad tempered men in your club, no matter how noted as players they may be. Leave them out, for they will eventually do more injury to a club than benefit.

We append the Constitution and By-Laws of the National Club, of Washington, as a good model to copy from in organizing a new Club. They are as follows:

CONSTITUTION.

ARTICLE I.

SEC. 1. This Club shall be known as the " National Base Ball Club of Washington;" and the objects of the Club shall be to " improve, foster and perpetuate the American game of Base Ball," and advance morally, socially, and physically, the interests of its members.

ARTICLE II.

SEC. 1. Candidates for membership must be proposed in writing, to the Board of Directors, by a member of the Club, setting forth the name and address of the candidate, and be signed by the member offering the same.

SEC. 2. Such proposition must be accompanied with the

initiation fee and annual dues, and be before the Board at least one week for consideration. The Directors shall report the same at the next meeting of the Club thereafter, with their opinions thereon, and the candidate must then be balloted for; and if no more than one-third of the members dissent, he shall be declared elected.

SEC. 3. Honorary members may be elected by a unanimous vote at any regular meeting of the Club.

SEC. 4. Any member desiring to withdraw from the Club shall offer his resignation in writing, at a regular meeting, and such resignation may be accepted if the member be not in arrears.

SEC. 5. Any member who shall make himself obnoxious, or be guilty of disreputable conduct, or violate any of the rules and regulations of the Club, may by a two-third vote at any regular meeting be expelled, suspended, reprimanded or fined.

ARTICLE III.

OFFICERS.

SEC. 1. The officers of this Club shall consist of a President, Vice-President, Secretary, Treasurer, and a Board of five Directors, " one of whom shall be the President," who shall be elected on the first Monday of March in each year, and shall hold their offices for one year, or until their successors are respectively elected.

SEC. 2. Each " officer," shall be elected by ballot separately, and must receive a majority of all the votes cast.

SEC. 3. The Board of Directors may be balloted for conjointly, and the four candidates receiving the greatest number of votes cast shall be declared elected.

SEC. 4. In case of vacancy in any office by reason of resignation of any officer, or for any other cause, the same shall be filled at a regular meeting.

ARTICLE IV.

DUTIES OF OFFICERS.

SEC. 1.   It shall be the duty of the President to preside at all meetings of the Club, preserve order, and appoint all committees not otherwise provided for.

SEC. 2.   The Vice-President shall perform all the duties of the President in his absence.

SEC. 3.   The Secretary shall keep a correct record of the proceedings of the Club, notify members of all special meetings, and keep a correct register of the members, with their places of business or residence.   He shall keep a debit and credit account with each member, shall receive all moneys paid to the Club, and report the amount of the same at any regular meeting, and hand the same to the Treasurer, taking his receipt therefor.   He shall also prepare, and caused to be published, notices of meetings, match games, and such other matter as may be ordered by the Directors.

SEC. 4.   The Treasurer shall keep in a suitable book an account of all money received and paid;   shall pay all bills against the Club, when instructed so to do by the Board of Directors, or by a vote of the Club, and when called upon shall state the amount of funds on hand "at any regular meeting."

SEC. 5.   The Directors shall provide all implements required by the Club, and suitable grounds for exercise; they shall audit all bills against the Club, and when correct direct the payment of the same by written order on the Treasurer.   When any match shall have been agreed on by the Club, they shall select the nines, appoint captains, and have entire control of the same, and make all necessary arrangements therefor; they shall place no player on the first nine who refuses to play on any inferior nine. (The *best* plan, however, in managing the nine of a club, is, to appoint a Captain for the season giving him entire control of the nine and holding him responsible for the result of the season's play.)

ARTICLE V.

INITIATION FEE, DUES, ETC.

SEC. 1. Each member shall pay "on joining," as an initiation fee, the sum of *five dollars.*

SEC. 2. The annual dues shall be five dollars, payable in advance, on or before the first regular meeting in May. Members joining after the month of June will pay *pro rata* of the above dues.

SEC. 2. No member in arrears, or who has continued in arrears for the period of thirty days, (after 1st May,) shall be allowed to participate in any game or meeting of the Club, and if not then settled, his name shall be erased from the Club Books.

SEC. 4. Should the funds of this Club at any time become exhausted, there shall be an equal assessment on each member to obtain such sum as may be required ; such assessment to be made by a majority of the members present at a regular meeting.

ARTICLE VI.

MEETINGS.

SEC. 1. There shall be an annual meeting of the Club on the first Monday of March in each year, and a regular meeting on the first Monday of each month, at such place as the President shall designate; and all meetings shall commence at 7 1-2 o'clock P. M.

SEC. 2. The President may call special meetings for business when he shall deem it necessary, and also at the written request of any five members.

SEC. 3. Seven members shall constitute a quorum for the transaction of business at any meeting.

SEC. 4. The regular meetings for field exercise shall be on Monday, Wednesday and Friday, of each week during the season, at such hour as the Directors may designate.

SEC. 5. There shall be a practice game between the

first and second nines one day of each week, at such time as the Directors may designate.

ARTICLE VII.

AMENDMENTS.

SEC. 1. No alteration or amendment of this Constitution, or the by-laws herewith of this Club, shall be made except by a two-third vote of all the members present at a regular meeting; nor then, unless such alteration or amendment shall have been submitted in writing at a regular meeting at least one month previous to its adoption.

BY-LAWS.

ARTICLE 1.

RULES AND REGULATIONS FOR FIELD EXERCISE.

SEC. 1. This Club shall be governed by the following rules and regulations in all exercise games:

Rule 1. When assembled for field exercise the presiding officer shall appoint a scorer, and designate two members as captains, who shall retire and make up the game to be played, and shall observe at the same time that the players put opposite to each other should be as nearly equal as possible. The choice of sides shall then be tossed for; and the first "at the bat," shall be decided in like manner.

Rule 2. In making up a game for exercise, if there are fourteen or more players of this Club present on the field, no other persons, not members of this Club, shall be chosen in; but if there are not fourteen members present, the members of other Clubs may be chosen in to make up eighteen players in all.

Rule 3. Members appearing after the game has commenced, shall not be chosen in if there is no vacancy, or the sides full.

Rule 4. The scorer shall keep the game in a book provided for that purpose, and shall note all violations of the by-laws, rules and regulations, during exercise. He shall decide all disputes and differences relative to the game in the absence of the Umpire, from which decision there shall be no appeal. (Clubs should also make it the duty of the scorer to keep a file of every first nine game played with Association Club, in order that data may be furnished for making up the season's averages.)

Rule 5. The captains shall have absolute direction of their sides, and shall designate the position each player shall occupy in the field, which cannot be changed without their consent.

Sec. 2. All exercise and match games shall be governed by the rules and regulations adopted by the National Convention of Base Ball Clubs held in the City of New York.

ARTICLE II.

RESTRICTIONS.

Sec. 1. It shall not be "lawful," and shall be deemed to be a violation of these By-laws—

For any member to use improper or profane language at *any* meeting of the Club, or during the progress of any game;

For wearing or using the apparel of a fellow member without his permission;

For disputing the decision of an Umpire during field exercise;

For audibly expressing his opinion on a doubtful play before the decision of an Umpire is given;

For refusing to obey his captain in the exercise of his lawful authority;

For leaving a meeting, when assembled for business or exercise, without the permission of the presiding officer.

ARTICLE III.

ORDER OF BUSINESS.

1. Reading of minutes.
2. Reports of officers.
3. Reports of committees.
4. Election of officers.
5. Election of members.
6. Dues and finances.
7. Unfinished business.
8. Miscellaneous business.
9. Adjournment.

The order of business as above arranged may at any time, for an occasion, be changed or dispensed with by a two-third vote of the members present at a meeting.

Parliamentary rules shall be observed at all meetings of the Club.

THE CAPTAIN OF A NINE.

ONE of the rules governing the selections of an Umpire applies with equal force to the choice of a captain of a nine, viz: that it does not follow that because a man is a first class player—the best in the nine perhaps—that he is therefore the man to act as captain of the nine. We know of many an excellent player totally unfitted for the onerous position of captain of a nine. In the selection of a captain two classes of players are to be avoided, the one including those of quick temper, without self-control, dictatorial in their manner, imperious in commanding, and too fond of having this and that done simply because it is their desire that it should be so. The other class are those easily influenced, of no determination of character, afraid of censure, and too desirous of pleasing their friends, in the course they pursue, at the cost of the best interests of the nine they have in charge, or of the club they belong to.

THE QUALIFICATIONS OF A CAPTAIN.

The captain of a nine should be a good general player, and if he excels as a catcher all the better, for that is his place in the field; but he should be one able to excel in one or other of the positions of the in-field. His moral qualifications should certainly include self-control, quickness of observation, good judgment, determination of character, a manly love of fair play, and gentlemanly deportment to the extent at least of keeping silent when accidental errors are committed by the fielders, and also in regard to the manner in which he issues his orders to his nine. His physical requisites should include the ability to occupy any position in the field creditably in case of an emergency. But especially is it necessary that the captain of a nine should be well up in all the "points," of the game, and on the watch to take the advantage of the errors of the opposing nine, and he should also be well posted in strategy, and especially be proof against despondency when the odds are against him in a match and fortune frowns on him.

HOW TO MANAGE A NINE.

To get a nine into good working condition is a task requiring patience, perseverance, good humor, sound judgment and the determined spirit which overcomes all ordinary obstacles. In getting your nine together for the season first get your pitcher, and if you have any choice left, you should always select the man having the *most command of the ball in delivery*. Never mind what his speed or twist is, so long as he can command the ball so as to deliver it within a few inches of the spot aimed at. Having this command he is good enough to be the pitcher of a good supporting field, without it he is but a second-class man in the position even if he be the swiftest pitcher in the country. Next look for a good catcher, one who is not afraid of a ball and who can throw straight and keep his temper. Of all places in the field the catcher's position is the last for a

quick tempered man.   In fact, such a man has no place in
a ball field at all, but least of all behind.   In choosing your
basemen, let the man on the first base be one fearless and
sure in holding the hottest kind of thrown balls: and the
man on the third base equally fearless in facing swiftly batted balls, and also capable of throwing swiftly and accurately
to first base; and let the second base man be the most active
fielder of the three, and a good judge of a catch.   In selecting your short-stop let him be an accurate thrower to
begin with, but especially should he be noted for his activity
in backing up every player in the in-field as occasion may
require.   The short-stop should always be on the move
and on the look out, first behind third base, then running
home to help the catcher, anon playing second base, and
even running out to long field for a high ball.   See that
your out fielders are good at long throws and sure in
judging and catching fly balls, besides being active in supporting each other.   It shows either poor management or
a poor player to see any man of the nine standing still in
his position while the ball is on the move either in the air
or along the ground.   Remember that no nine is complete
without two pitchers in it, each different and opposite in
their styles of delivery.

ORDER OF STRIKING.

In practising your nine together in the early part of a
season, note particularly their peculiar styles of batting, and
according to these peculiarities fix upon their order of
striking, and keep them through the season in the same
order.   Many bases and runs are lost in the games of a
season by clubs who pay no attention to a regular order
of striking.   The advantages of this regular and perma-
nent order of striking are so palpable that it is a wonder
that first class clubs have neglected it for so many years.   It
is but comparatively a few seasons ago that nearly every
match of a nine was marked not only by a different order
of striking for each game, but also by changes of

positions in nearly every innings. In arranging your order of striking see that strong hitters follow the poor batsman, and that good base runners precede them. For instance, suppose that your best out-fielder or your pitcher or catcher is not as skillful at the bat as the others, in placing him on the books as a striker put a good base-runner's name down before him, and a good hitter after him, by this means the chances for the first base being vacated by the time he is ready to make it, will be increased, as likewise those for two runs being obtained after he has made his base. Never put three first class men together but let them face the pitcher alternately. Neither put three poor hitters together, but support each if possible as above recommended. Let your first striker always be the coolest hand of the nine.

CHANGING POSITIONS.

One of the now obsolete customs of a match game of ball used to be the change of positions in the field in nearly every innings. As a general thing this is the merest child's play. In the early part of the season, when engaged in an unimportant match with a weaker nine, a change or two may be allowable by way of experiment, but under no other circumstances, except those of illness or injury, should a position in the nine—except that of pitcher—be changed during the playing of a match, or, in fact, during the entire season, unless you can substitute a palpably superior player, or in case experience proves the inability of any one man to properly play his position in a nine. The folly of taking a base-player off his base, because he fails to hold a ball or too badly thrown or swiftly batted to him; or of putting a base player in the field because the fielder happens to drop a difficult ball to hold, or even to miss an easy catch, is so apparent to any ordinary observer that we are surprised to see it adopted by any but captains of weak judgment. What reason have you to suppose that the player committing an error in one position, and that, too, one he is familiar with, is going to do better in one he is not at home in, and if he does not, whence the advantage of the change? for, as the game is now played, every position in the field requires to be equally well played to insure success in a match. There is one change, however, that is legitimate and frequently advantageous, and that is,

A CHANGE OF PITCHERS.

In the management of your nine nothing shows your possession of good judgment more than your tactics in regard to the pitching department. In the first place, a first class team always has two pitchers in it, and it is in your management of these batteries that much of your success will lie. Put your swift pitcher to work first, and keep him in at least three innings, even if he be hit away from the start; for it will require that time to allow your opponents to become accustomed to the range of the balls, and therefore they will be more likely to strike too quick for a slower delivery when a change is made. In reference to a change of pitching we pre-suppose a proper support of the pitching in the field; should the pitcher not be supported well, however no change is likely to be of benefit, especially one of from swift to slow pitching, the effectiveness of slow pitching depending greatly upon the skill displayed by the field in making catches. Supposing, however, that with good support in the field the swift pitching is being easily punished, and runs are being made too fast, if your pitcher is one who cannot drop his pace well without giving more chances at the bat, you should at once bring in your slow or medium-paced pitcher, and at the same time prepare your field for catches by placing your basemen out further, letting the short-stop nearly cover second base, and the second base-man play at right short well out, and extending your out-fielders about ten yards or so. Your slow pitcher should be an active fielder, as he will have to cover the in-field well, for the basemen will have to lay out well for high balls between the in-field and the out-field. If your changed pitcher can now and then send in a hot one without any apparent change of delivery, his pitching will be all the more effective; when he does so, however, he should draw in his basemen closer by private signal. Always have an understanding with your two sets of fielders in regard to private signals, so as to be able to call them in closer, or place them out further, or nearer the foul ball lines, as occasion may require without giving notice to your adversaries. Warn your out-fielders also to watch well the batsman so as to be ready to move in the direction he faces for batting. Thus if the left-fielder is in his regular position and he sees the batsman facing for a hit close to the first base let understanding him go nearer to centre-field, and the centre-fielder nearer to right, and the latter fielder close to if not beyond the foul ball line. When you find that your adversaries have in their nine two or three men fond of making showy hits or of hitting at the first ball that comes to them as hard as they can, lay your out-field in readiness for long fly balls; extend your basemen for high balls short of the out-field, and then tell your pitcher to send him in a nice one where he wants it, and in nine cases out of ten if your men are well trained the " splendidly hit ball " will be held as nicely as you want it. Be careful, however, that you are not tempted to draw in your men too much for low hits; you should consult with your pitcher every innings so as to have the nine work according to his pitching. In fact the pitcher should be allowed to place his men if he have any special object in view, or desires to play any particular points. It is in paying particular attentions to the strategetical points of a game that victories are achieved, and not in depending solely on your strength either at the bat or in the field.

A NINE AT THE BAT.

In managing your nine at the bat see that the striker is not teased by others of the nine into hitting at a ball that does not suit him. Nothing is more annoying to a bats

man than to have two or three calling out to him to wait
for this ball, or to hit at that, or not to hit at another, and
so on.   Every man knows what ball he wants and should
be allowed to use his own judgment.   If the position of the
game requires that the striker should either be more particular then usual in selecting a ball, or less so, let him be
quietly posted on the subject before he takes his stand, or
otherwise you expose your hand to your opponent.   Nothing
bothers a field more than for batsmen to follow up a good
hit by striking quickly in succession and running the
bases rapidly.   In such cases extra risks may be taken, especially when two bases are occupied, for the result of two
or three sharp hits in succession is to discourage the pitcher, get him excited and the field confused.   Consider that
you have always gained a point and a good one two, when
you have got your opponents growling at each other in the
field, for nothing tends to demoralize a nine more than
fault finding at just such periods of a game as this.   Many
a brilliant rally—the result of following up a lucky hit
with quick play at the bat—has led nines to victory where
defeat would certainly have ensued had the opposing nine
in the field preserved their coolness and judgment instead of losing their tempers and their presence of mind.
Watch the movements of the fielders and warn your batsmen accordingly.   When a change of pitching is made
from fast to slow put your batsman on their guard so that
they may make a change in timing the ball.   If the
pitching is from slow to swift, shorten your hold of the bat
and take a shorter swing.   If from fast to slow hold your
bat close to the handle and take a wider range in swinging, by this means you will time your swing so as to
meet the ball at the right place.   Insist upon your men
running to first base with all their speed the moment they
hit the ball, no matter how or where it be sent.   The habit
of stopping running because a ball is "sure to be
caught or for a foul ball," etc., is a very bad one, and has
lost many a player his first base.

In conclusion we would say to every captain never to forget to speak to his men as he would like to be spoken to by a captain himself. Keep up discipline but let respect and regard for you be the main incentives to obedience by your men. We trust all captains will observe the good old custom of closing a game with mutual cheers for each other's club, and a field cheer for the Umpire, for it is a custom calculated to promote good feeling between the players.

CHAMPIONSHIP GAMES.

THE title of " Champion Club," is one not recognized by the National Association, and it is one that is not advisable for the interests of the game at large that it should be. As there are a number of clubs, however, anxious to win the coveted title, and as it has been an aid to the game in extending it in popularity in country districts—though it has had the reverse effect in large cities and towns—we have, at the request of several clubs, prepared a series of rules for the government of this class of contests in such localities as have no regular code for a guide, such as the clubs of several places have adopted—New England for instance.

WHAT CONSTITUTES A CHAMPION CLUB.

The title of " champion club of the United States," becomes a less and less legitimate title every year. When base ball was comparatively unknown outside of the Middle States, and New York was the central point of the game, it was not difficult for a club to become the champion organization, as the strongest clubs were located within a circuit of twenty miles around New York city; but as the game spread, and strong clubs began to show themselves, first in Pennsylvania, then in New England, then in Washington, and so on in other States and districts, the circle became enlarged, and the question began to assume a different phase, until now we have a half dozen clubs of different localities so nearly equal in strength that the close of the season of 1866 left the question of the championship in such an undecided state that it is difficult to state which is now the champion club, and which is not. Of course as the game is extended more and more in popularity, and the distance between different sections of the country, in which it prevails, prevents meetings between rival contestants for the palm of superiority, the question as to which is the champion club of the country will become more and more difficult to answer; but not so in regard to the clubs entitled to the coveted laurels as the strongest playing club in each State; that question can always be readily answered. Thus the Athletic Club is, undoubtedly, the champion of Pennsylvania; the Lowell Club of Massachusetts; the Charter Oak of Connecticut; the Eureka of New Jersey; the National of the District of Columbia, etc., etc. It should be remembered that the title of champion club only extends from season to season, thus one club may be champions one year and another club the next. The Eckford Club were the champions in 1862–3, and the Atlantics in 1864–5 and '6, for though the Atlantics did not win either every game they played, or even every series of games, the fact that they were not defeated in any series of games, best two out of three, allows them to retain the title until so defeated, of course, provided they accept every legitimate challenge sent them within the period constituting the season, viz : in New York from May 1st, until Thanksgiving day in November.

The club most legitimately entitled to the honors of the championship is that one which wins every game they play during a season, and that too against the strongest club they can induce to meet them. No club either before or since has equalled the career of the Eckford Club of Brooklyn, in 1863, in which year they won every first nine, second nine, and amateur game they played, including contests with the strongest clubs of Brooklyn, New York and Newark, etc. Previous to that time (the seasons of 1862-3) the Atlantics held the championship streamer, and since then too they have retained it. The season of 1867, may, however, place the " whip " in other hands.

RULES FOR CHAMPIONSHIP CONTESTS.

In districts or States where no code of rules exist the following will be found correct as a code of rules for championship games:

Rule 1st. A club must win every series of games—viz: best two out of three—they play during each year in order to win the title of champion club; and in order to retain it they must not be defeated in any such series of games.

Rule 2d. The champion club must accept every legitimate challenge sent them during the period known as the base ball season; provided the challenge sent them does not emanate from a club which has been defeated by another club previously defeated the same year by the challenged club.

Rule 3d. Every first nine game played by the champion club is to count as a championship game without regard to notice thereof in the challenge or announcement.

Rule 4th. One week's notice is the shortest time allowable for notices or challenges for championship games.

Rule 5th. No champion club can be obliged to play more than one match a week.

Rule 6th. A written challenge or acceptance of one, from the Secretary of one club to that of another alone holds good.

Rule 7th. A written challenge, accepted in writing, binds to a game being played or a ball forfeited, unless withdrawn by mutual consent.

Rule 8th. A challenge dates from the time of its deposite in the Post Office.

Rule 9th. Any man, taking part in a regular match game of a club, shall be regarded as a regular member of the club he plays with, as far as such membership concerns his playing in another club, no matter whether he has signed the constitution, paid dues or not.

Rule 10*th.* The champion club of the United States is not bound to play any club not belonging to the National Association; and no champion club of a State or City is bound to play any club not belonging either to the National Association of the State or the parent organization.

Rule 11*th.* The base ball season, or period within which challenges are legitimate or otherwise differs in regard to its extent according to the section of the country in which the challenged club is located. Thus in New York it it is from May to November. In the Southwest, from April to November. In the South from January to December, and so on.

ON PITCHING.

THE position of pitcher, in base ball, is the most important in the nine, as on his ability depends much of the success of a nine in a match. It does not follow, however, that because the pitcher of a nine is a first class one that therefore the nine will win; or, that because he happens to be a poor player in the position that defeat must necessarily be the result; for excellent support in the field will frequently offset the weakness of the pitcher, while we have seen Creighton's pitching nullified by the lack of good support from the field. But as a general thing, all other things being equal, a good pitcher in a nine is a *sine qua non* in achieving success.

Before proceeding further, we give the rules which govern the pitcher.

THE PITCHER'S POSITION.

SEC. 5. The pitcher's position shall be designated by two lines, yards in length, drawn at right angles to a

line from home to second base, having their centres upon
that line at two fixed iron plates, placed at points fifteen
and sixteen and one-third yards distant from the home
base. The pitcher must stand within the lines, and must
deliver the ball as near as possible over the centre of the
home base, and fairly for the striker.

DELIVERING UNFAIR BALLS.

Sec. 6. Should the pitcher *repeatedly* fail to deliver to
the striker fair balls, for the apparent purpose of delaying
the game, or for any cause, the Umpire, after *warning
him*, shall call one ball, and if the pitcher *persists* in such
action, two and three balls; when three balls shall have
been called, the striker shall take the first base; and should
any base be occupied at that time, each player occupying
it or them shall take one base without being put out. All
balls delivered by the pitcher, striking the ground before
reaching the line of the home base, or pitched over the
head of the batsman, or pitched to the side opposite to that
which the batsman strikes from, shall be considered unfair
balls.

BALKING.

Sec. 7. The ball must be pitched, not jerked or thrown
to the bat; and whenever the pitcher moves with the apparent purpose or pretention to deliver the ball, he shall so
deliver it, and must have neither foot in advance of the
front line or off the ground at the time of delivering the
ball; and if he fails in either of these particulars then it
shall be declared a balk. The ball should be considered
as *jerked*, in the meaning of the rule, if the pitcher's arm
touches his person when the arm is swung forward to deliver the ball; and it shall be regarded as a *throw* if the
arm be bent at the elbow, at an angle from the body, or
horizontally from the shoulder when it is swung forward
to deliver the ball. A *pitched* ball is one delivered with
the *arm straight and swinging perpendicularly*, and free
from the body.

BALKED AND CALLED BALLS DEAD.

SEC. 10. Any ball delivered by the pitcher on which a balk or a ball has been called, shall be considered *dead* and not in play until it has been settled in the hands of the pitcher *while he stands within the lines of his position* and no such ball, if hit, shall put the striker out.

RUNNING BASES, OR FOUL BALLS.

SEC. 19. No ace or base can be made upon a foul ball; such a ball shall be considered dead, and not in play until it shall first have been *settled in the hands of the pitcher.* In such cases players running bases shall return to them, and may be put out in so returning, in the same manner as the striker when running to the first base.

BALLS STOPPED BY OUTSIDERS.

SEC. 26. If an adversary stops the ball with his hat or cap, or if a ball be stopped by any person not engaged in the game, or if it be taken from the hands of any one not engaged in the game, no player can be put out unless the ball shall first have settled in the hands of the pitcher *while he stands within the lines of his position.*

The above are all the rules governing the movements of the pitcher; and from them he learns, first, that his position occupies a space of ground six feet by four, within which space he must stand in delivering the ball to the bat, and also in receiving the ball from the field in the case of delivering a balked or called ball, and also when the ball has been stopped by the crowd of spectators. Secondly, that he is also required to keep both feet on the ground when he swings his arm forward in delivering the ball—and he observes the rule properly if his toes only touch the ground. And thirdly, that in delivering the ball he is required to pitch the ball over the home base and "*fairly for the striker,*" a fair delivery for the striker meaning balls sent within the *legitimate* reach of the batsman, this legitimate reach being bounded by the length of his bat from him, within a foot of the ground, and on a line with his head, a space sufficiently extensive for any pitcher, possessing only ordinary accuracy of aim and command of the ball, to pitch according to the rules.

THE REQUISITES OF A PITCHER.

The one essential point in pitching is, *command of the ball.* A pitcher may have speed and endurance, but without command of the ball in delivery he lacks the most important element of success in pitching. The power to pitch swiftly is also an important requisite, and the ability to impart a bias or "twist," to the ball, which is simply causing the ball to revolve on its own axis either to the right or the left on its passage from the hand to the bat is considered a desirable point. With thorough command of the ball a pitcher can do without speed or even the endurance to pitch through nine innings, and yet prove a troublesome pitcher to his opponents. But, he may have speed and the power to last through a long game, and yet his lack of control of the ball in delivery will so nullify his other advantages as to render his efforts to win a complete failure, his pitching, under such circumstances, costing more in called and passed balls—from lack of accuracy of delivery—than it yields in tips or poorly hit balls. A first class pitcher therefore should first possess the ability to pitch a ball within a few inches of the spot he aims for; secondly, the power to pitch a very swift ball, and thirdly to have the strength to endure the fatigue of pitching through a long game. Add to these requisite qualifications the judgment to pitch according to the batsmen's peculiarities who stand before him, and the skill to deceive him as much as possible as to the character of the ball pitched to him, and the pitcher will then have all the ability to become a second Creighton as far as pitching is concerned.

THE LINES OF THE BALL IN PITCHING.

The difficulty in fairly hitting a pitched ball is increased or decreased according as the line of its direction is

curved or straightened. A thrown ball, for instance,
which goes from the hand to the bat almost in a straight
line, is easier to hit than a tossed ball, from the fact that in
the former case you have the whole length of the line to
judge the ball in, whereas in the curved line you have but
a foot or two of the line of the ball to judge it. The following diagrams illustrate this :

The line of A Thrown Ball, with the Lines of the Bat.

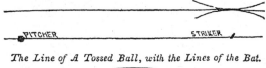

The Line of A Tossed Ball, with the Lines of the Bat.

It will be seen, in the above diagrams, that in the case
of the thrown ball the lines of the bat closely intersect
the line of the ball, thereby affording the bat a chance of
hitting the ball nearly the length of its full swing; but in
the case of the curved line of the slowly pitched ball—viz:
a tossed ball—the lines of the bat intersect it almost at
right angles thereby allowing of but a slight chance to hit
the ball. It will be readily seen from these illustrations
that curved lines in pitching are the most difficult for the
batsman to judge, and consequently a primary object to
be attained in pitching is, to obtain as much of a
curve, in the line of the ball in delivery, as the speed required will admit of.

Next to curved lines in pitching comes the point of
causing the ball to rise to the bat when pitched swiftly.

By this means the eye of the batsman is greatly deceived. and he is very apt to strike over the ball in nearly every instance. To obtain this rise, the ball, in pitching, should leave the hand within a few inches of the ground; the nearer the hip of the pitcher the ball leaves him the straighter the line will be, and consequently the lower it can be pitched the better. The ball can thus leave the hand close to the ground and yet rise to the shoulder of the batsman if necessary. The difference in the effect of these lines is shown in the following diagrams :

The Line of a High Delivery.

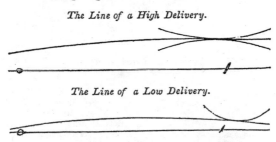

The Line of a Low Delivery.

It will be seen that in the case of the high delivery that the lines of the bat intersect the line of the ball in such a manner as to greatly increase the chances of hitting the ball; whereas in the low delivery the lines of the bat, both from a shoulder-strike as well as from a horizontal swing, have but a few inches to interersect the line of the ball; thereby decreasing the chances of hitting the ball fairly. These lines are those of swiftly-pitched balls, the rule being that the greater the speed the less the curve.

When the batsman requires a low ball, more speed is requisite in the delivery. The reason of this is that in striking at a low ball, the line of the bat forms a section of a circle and in this instance the greater the curve the better the chance of the ball being hit, as will be seen by the following diagrams :

A Fast Low Ball.

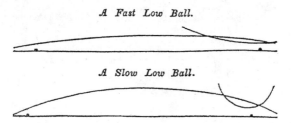

A Slow Low Ball.

In the first case the line of the bat intersects the line of the ball in the course of its swing at but two places, and then at an acute angle, while in the other case the line of the bat follows that of the ball quite a distance.

The following are the lines of the four classes of balls generally called for, viz : *shoulder high*, *hip high*, *knee high* and "*a low ball*." The latter should never be less than a foot from the ground, all balls, lower than that not being within the legitimate reach of the batsman, and therefore unfair both as to delivery and as to being called for, the batsman having no more right to call for a ball out of the circle of a legitimate reach than the pitcher has to deliver such a one when not called for.

A Ball Shoulder High.

A Ball Hip High.

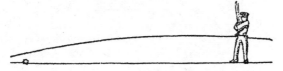

A Ball Knee High.

A Low Ball.

Below we give the lines of swiftly pitched balls; of medium paced, of "slows," and of tossed balls:

A Swiftly Pitched Ball.

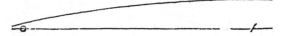

A Medium Paced Ball.

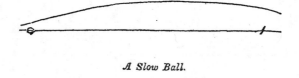

A Slow Ball.

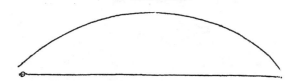

A Tossed Ball.

DELIVERING THE BALL.

The fewer movements a pitcher has in delivering the ball the better. His chances of balking are less, for one thing, while his opportunities for deceiving the batsman and the base runner are greater. The great objective point of the pitcher is to deceive the eye and judgment of the batsman, so as to cause him to strike too quick or too slow at the ball to hit it squarely, and to gain this point successfully the pitcher should deliver the ball with as few movements as possible.

THE PITCHER'S POSITION.

The following cut represents the position of the pitcher preparatory to delivering the ball :

PRELIMINARY MOTIONS.

No pitcher can well have less than three motions in delivering the ball, and no one ought to have more. These are, first, bending the body; second, drawing the arm back; and third, swinging it forward to deliver the ball. If in making these three motions he can at the same time send in the ball swiftly or slowly, as occasion may require, without perceptibly changing his movement in delivery, he will have achieved quite a point in pitching, one which has more to do with making a pitcher effective than any thing else short of acquiring perfect command of the ball. The importance of having as few motions in delivery as possible is shown in the fact that thereby the chances of making balks are decreased, and, also, but a few chances are offered to base runners in stealing bases on the pitcher. The pitcher should not be hurried in his movements but should husband his strength by being as deliberate in his motions as he can without being lazy, at the same time his style of delivery should be rapid as far as the several movements he makes in pitching the ball are concerned. It should be remembered that a balk dates from the time that the pitcher makes one of the movements peculiar to him in delivering the ball, and fails to follow it up by actual delivery to the bat.

WHAT CONSTITUTES A BALK.

A balk is made, when the pitcher makes a motion to deliver the ball and fails to deliver it; also when he has either foot outside the lines of his position, or when he lifts either foot *entirely* off the ground before the ball is on its way to the bat. For instance, first in regard to making a motion to deliver. The pitcher we will say, has three movements preliminary to pitching, viz : to bend his body, draw his arm back, and then swing it forward. Now, if he commences to bend his body, as in the first motion of his regular delivery, and then stops to look round he makes a balk, just the same as if he were to stop after drawing his arm back or after swinging it forward. Of course, the same rule holds good if he have more than three regular movements, the balk being dated from the very first of the series of movements the pitcher is in the habit of making in delivery, unless the same be promptly followed up by actual delivery to the bat. Secondly, in regard to having his feet outside the lines. If the pitcher steps *over* the lines of his position in pitching, either with the forward foot or hind foot, he makes a balk. Thirdly, in reference to lifting his feet. The rule requires that the pitcher shall have both feet on the ground while he is in the act of pitching the ball, and if he lift either foot entirely off the ground—it does not matter if he lifts his heel or toe, provided some portion of his foot is on the ground—before the ball has plainly left his hand, then he makes a balk. Of course, if he either throws or jerks a ball the same becomes a balk; and if his arm touch his body when it is swung forward in delivery, it is considered as a jerk, and if his arm be bent at the elbow at an angle from the body, or if it does not swing straight and perpendicular in delivery it is considered as a thrown ball and a balk in each case is called.

GIVING A BIAS TO THE BALL.

A very high estimate has hitherto been placed upon the ability of a pitcher to impart a bias or "twist," to the ball as it leaves his hand; that is giving it a rotary motion, either to the right or left, on its own axis, while on its way to the bat. It is more than questionable, however, whether it is of any use in pitching in base ball, inasmuch as the direction of the ball from the bat, whether foul or fair, high or low, depends mainly upon the position in which the ball touches the bat, rather than upon the effect of any bias imparted to the ball by the pitcher. For instance if the ball be hit by the bat—as seen in the annexed diagram—it will leave the bat in a line in exact accordance with the line of the bat swung to meet it, no matter what rotary motion the ball may have had imparted to it by the pitcher.

A Squarely Hit Ball.

If the ball also be hit in the manner shown in the following diagram it will go from the bat foul with or without a twist from the pitcher :

A Foul Tipped Ball.

Should the ball, striking the bat as in the above diagram, have a forward rotary motion imparted to it—not to the right or to the left—it would of course be of assistance in causing it to leave the bat at an angle different from that without it, but this would yield no advantage.

In fact it is questionable whether the twist to the right or left, given to the ball is not rather a disadvantage than otherwise, and for this reason : A ball to which a rotary motion has been given by the pitcher, the moment it strikes the ground rebounds at an angle to the right or left according to the motion it has had imparted to it, and this change of direction chiefly results from its striking the ground, and its only effect is to bother the catcher in judging of the rebound. When the ball is struck by the bat above or below its centre, then, too, it feels the effect of the bias imparted to it, the result, as before, being to make its direction more difficult to judge; but if hit squarely by the bat, then, as we have before shown, the bias imparted to the ball by the pitcher has little or no effect until the ball strikes the ground after having been sent from the bat. Much of the poor hitting resulting from curved lines in medium-paced and slow pitching, and also from very swift pitching, has been credited to "twist," in the ball, when the failure to hit the ball squarely has been the real cause of the poor batting. In bowling in cricket, of course, the giving a bias to the ball is half the battle, but in pitching in base ball an examination into the philosophy of the thing will be very likely to show that twisting a ball is a point in pitching of far less consequence than it has hitherto been considered by the fraternity.

HEADWORK IN PITCHING.

"Headwork," is the technical phrase used in base ball in reference to pitching with sound judgment. It is a comprehensive term and embraces coolness of calculation in estimating the skill of your opponent at the bat, the judgment to pitch the ball so as to deceive him as much as possible, and the ability to avail yourself of all his weak points, such as pitching him a ball on which he can make a favorite hit, after you had quietly placed a man to catch it, or in apparently sending him a ball where he wants it, though in reality one is sent where he cannot strike it, &c. A pitcher who simply brings to bear his physical qualifications in a match will find the nine he pitches for a defeated party if his opponent in handling the ball is one who can use his head in pitching as well as his hands. We have frequently seen a pitcher, having command of the ball, together with the requisite speed and endurance, send ball after ball in, which were hit away by batsmen whom a pitcher, using his wits as well as his arm, would have caused to retire from the bat with blank scores again and again. A really effective pitcher studies his men just as a prize fighter does his stronger and bigger but less experienced adversary. He does not send in ball after ball at hazard, but endeavors to ascertain the calibre of his man and having found out his strong and weak points he pitches accordingly. Any one who does not do this is not a first class pitcher, no matter how fast or accurate he may pitch or how long he can last in a game.

PLAYING POINTS.

A first-class pitcher has two men whom he finds it a special part of his business to deceive viz : the Batsman and the Umpire. The one is much easier "done" than the other, as a general thing. The batsman is to be led into error by pitching; the Umpire is to be hoodwinked by talking. When we say deceive, we simply mean to get the batsman and Umpire confused or bothered, so that in the one case poor hits are made, and in the other the pitcher escapes half the penalties a strict interpretation of the rules would have inflicted upon him. Let us give an illustration of these two "points :" A batsman takes his position cool and collected and just in time for a home run. He at once shows the pitcher the spot he wants a ball, quietly remarking "I want one just about there." Well, a ball comes in just the height he wants it, but too far off; another follows but this time it is too close in; again the ball comes but it is barely within range of his bat, although high enough each time; still again, it comes and once more is a little too close to him. All this time the balls have appeared to the crowd to be just the thing for the striker, as not a third of the spectators can see whether the ball is too close or too far off, although all can judge of the height of a ball, consequently as ball after ball comes in, in reality out of fair hitting distance, but apparently fair for the bat, the impatience of the crowd manifests itself, and the striker is tempted either to hit at a ball which does not suit him, or getting flurried misses the first good ball sent him; and it invariably happens that just as the striker, tired of waiting for the ball he wants, stands unprepared to strike, in comes the very ball he wanted, and "judgment" cries the pitcher, and "one strike," answers the Umpire when, had the latter done his duty, three balls would most likely have given the striker his base. But the pitcher has found out how far he can outwit the Umpire, and having gauged him he plays his cards accordingly. This is one phase of "headwork" in pitching, and also comes un-

der the head of "points." Again, by way of illustrating
another point. The pitcher, we will suppose, finds himself
faced by an old hand at the bat who can not be dodged into
striking at a poor ball, besides which the Umpire happens
to be a veteran at the business who is alike proof against
the dodgy tricks of the pitcher, so the latter has to resort
to another line of tactics, and first sending in a few tossed
balls or medium placed ones out of reach suddenly sends in
a hot one where the striker wants it but the latter, striking
too slow at it, either misses it or pops it up. Or if the pitcher finds the batsman too eager or too ready for a swift
ball, he as suddenly sends in a slow one, and the batsman
striking too quickly fails to hit it. This change of pace,
it should be remembered, is done so neatly that the batsman
cannot discover by the movements of the pitcher whether
a fast or a slow ball is coming until it is on the way to the
bat. As in cricket nothing bothers the batsman so much
as a fast bowler in one and a slow one the next, so in
base ball no pitching is so troublesome as that marked by
very swift balls and then slow ones, sent in according to
the state of preparation the batsman is in to meet them.
The pitcher should remember that though the rules require
him to pitch "fairly for the striker," the point of play in
his position is to learn how not to do that very thing, without showing the cloven foot, or in other words it should be
his policy to apparently pitch fair balls but in reality to
send them just where the batsman does not want them.
To do this skillfully, however, and in such a way as to
avoid the penalties of the law, requires that very amount
of skill included in the term of headwork.

An excellent opportunity to play points on a batsman is
afforded the pitcher when the batsman undertakes to wait
at the bat until his predecessor vacates the first base.
This waiting business is illegal, and the pitcher should
make it a point to appeal to the Umpire on every ball sent
in within the legitimate reach of the bat. It is the very
time, too, for him to send in balls the right height and as

near to the place indicated as he safely can do, for if this is done at the very outset, the pitcher will perhaps get two strikes out of his opponent, and the fear of a third will make him fidgety and consequently uncertain in his aim, a poor hit and the cutting off of the runner from first to second being a very likely result. As a general rule when you see the batsman inclined to wait when a player is on the first base, pitch him the ball he wants at once.

PITCHING FOR CATCHES.

A point in pitching, and one few pitchers make, is that of pitching balls for catches. When you see that the batsman has a favorite style of hitting and is anxious to get a ball on which he can make a home run, place your men properly for a fly ball and then toss him in a good one to hit up. You must be careful that it is not a ball he can send along the ground, though. You should also be careful to change your field in such a way that he will not notice it. Have an understanding with the three out-fielders and first and second basemen and short-stop, that at a certain signal they are to get well out into the field and when they are ready, drop in a "short one," and in nine cases out of ten the ball will go up and out into the field amid the cheers of the crowd only to drop into the hands of an expert out-fielder who was laying low for the very ball. The pitcher must bear in mind that he has something more to do in his position than merely to pitch the ball if he desires to excel as an effective pitcher.

SWIFT PITCHING.

Speed, as an element of success in pitching is alone useful when brought to bear against inexperienced batsmen, and when the pitcher has a good catcher to support him. A swift pitcher requires his catcher to stand up well and receive his punishment boldly, and especially to stop all balls, even it they happen to be too hot to hold neatly. As a general thing very swift pitching costs more in passed and called balls than it yields in tips and poor hits. A good pitcher, however, should be able to send in a pretty hot ball when necessary. The swiftest pitching can be readily hit by experienced batsmen; it is the happy combination of slow, medium-paced and swiftly pitched balls which proves to be the most troublesome style in the long run. Swift pitching came into vogue with the lamented Creighton, his brilliant success as a pitcher being attributed entirely to his speed, when his command of the ball and consequent accuracy of aim had more to do with the effectiveness of his pitching than anything else. The host of imitators who followed him led to the introduction of the era of fast pitching and "waiting games," an evil which was only put a stop to by the changes made in the rules of the National Association, by which, the penalty of calling balls was inflicted for unfair pitching, and more recently the much-needed reformation of describing unfair balls and defining fair pitching was introduced.

SLOW PITCHING.

The advantage of slow, or rather medium-paced pitching over a swift delivery, as a general rule in pitching is becoming every season more manifest. As Creighton was the exemplification of a swift pitcher, and the most effective of the class ever known, so Martin—of the Irving, Empire and Mutual clubs of New York successively—is now the best medium-paced pitcher of the country. In swift pitching the work in the field lays chiefly between the pitcher and catcher, the in-fielders only occasionally getting a little employment, the main dependence for success in the match being on the swift pitching. In medium-paced pitching, however, the reverse is the case, for it is on the excellence of the fielding that the success of the party adopting the medium-pace style depends. Hence, instead of the tedium of listening to the cry of "foul" or "three strikes out" from the Umpire, in a game marked by swift pitching, we have, in a contest in which the pace is sacrificed to "length"—(as the cricketers call a well-pitched ball)—a display in the field of the most attractive features of the game, the play in this latter instance affording ample opportunities for a development of fine fielding in the way of taking difficult fly balls, and in making beautiful stops, and accurate throws to bases, while all the attraction of double and treble plays are shown.

THE PITCHER AS A FIELDER.

One requisite of a first class pitcher is the ability to field well in the position. The pitcher frequently has the swiftest style of balls batted to him, and therefore he requires to be a pretty courageous fellow in order to face the ball well. He should also be an accurate thrower to the bases and learn to throw to them by signal from the catcher. In fact, this is the only effectual plan of catching a player napping on the bases, the style generally in vogue resulting too frequently in overthrown balls. The best way to play this point is to agree upon a certain movement made by the catcher as a signal to throw, and never to throw unless the signal is given. The player cannot watch the catcher and pitcher too, and if he sees the pitcher apparently not looking he will take liberties and get well off his base. A pitcher who is habitually deliberate in his movements will succeed in thus playing this point the best, as the player wont be put upon his guard by seeing the pitcher stopping before he pitches. Creighton and Leggett used to do this thing very successfully. The pitcher should remember the difference in the application of the rules in reference to his position, in which, in the case of foul balls, the ball is required to be settled in his hands—while he is standing any where in the field—before it becomes in play, but which in the case of a ball stopped by an outside crowd is to be settled in his hands *while he stands within the lines of his position*, before it is again in play. And this latter is also the case when a balk or a ball has been called, the ball being "dead" in each instance until he has held it in his position. In cases of foul balls, therefore, when a player is trying to get to a base the pitcher should run to the base the player is trying to get back to, and endeavor to hold the ball while on the base, before his opponent reaches it. In fielding a foul ball when a player is on a base, the pitcher should be careful not to hold it unless the base player is near his base in readiness to receive the ball from the pitcher. Many a base has been stolen by the negligence of a pitcher in this respect. When a player is on the third base too, and trying to run home, the pitcher should always follow up every ball passing the batsman. The position of the pitcher in delivering should be as upright a one as possible. He should stand firm in his position, too, taking a wide stride, for with his legs well apart and taking a springing movement partly on his toes he can give a great impetus to the swing of his arm in delivery, whereas if he stands with his legs nearly close together his movements will be necessarily cramped.

No nine in a club is complete unless it contains two men in it competent to act as pitchers. The one should excel as a fast pitcher, and the other's *forte* should be in slow or medium-paced balls. It so frequently happens that the entire aspect of a game is changed by the substitution of a slow for a fast pitcher, or a swift-delivery for a medium-paced one that it has become an established rule that a nine is not fully prepared for victory which has not two men in it able to fill the position of pitcher, and that, too, with each man having a style of delivery almost the opposite of the other.

When you have delivered a ball on which the Umpire calls a " balk " or a " ball," and there are any players running the bases, see that the ball so delivered be returned to your hands from the catcher—if the batsman misses it—or from the fielder if the ball be hit, as promptly as possible; for you must bear in mind that, though the ball be " dead " under such circumstances as far as the striker is concerned, it does not prevent base runners from making their bases. The ball, however, becomes in play again the moment you have held it while standing within the lines of your position, but not until then. The point, therefore, is to get it back from the fielder as soon as possible, and throw it at once to the baseman manning the base the runner is trying to reach. This is a new point in the game, resulting from the introduction of rule No. 10.

ON BATTING.

THE POSITION OF THE STRIKER.

The following are the rules governing the striker.:

"SEC 21. The striker, when in the act of striking, shall not step forward or backward, but must stand on a line drawn through the centre of the home base, not exceeding in length three feet from either side thereof, and parallel with the line occupied by the pitcher. He shall be considered the striker until he has struck a fair ball Players must strike in regular rotation, and, after the first innings is played, the turn commences with the player who stands on the list next to the one who lost the third hand.

"SEC. 42. Should a striker stand at the bat without striking at good balls repeatedly pitched to him, for the apparent purpose of delaying the game, or of giving advantage to a player, the Umpire, after warning him, shall call one strike, and if he persists in such action, two and three strikes. When three strikes are called he shall be subject to the same rules as if he had struck at three fair balls."

It will be seen by the above rules that the first thing the striker has to do in taking his position is, to place one foot upon the line of the base and keep it there until he has struck the ball. He should stand on the line in question, at least a foot from the base so as to allow the pitcher a chance to pitch over the base. Indeed it would be desirable for him to stand fully two feet from the base, and for the following reasons : should he stand close to the base the pitcher can send balls over the home base and that at the height the striker wants them, thereby obeying the law, and yet send in balls too close to the batsman to be hit well; and if he stánds too far from the base—say the full three feet—the pitcher can still pitch over the base and yet send the ball too far from the bat to be effectively hit. This line of the home base, it should be borne in mind, is one parallel to a line from first to third bases, and consequently does not allow of the batsman standing forward or backward of the home base, but simply on one side or the other of the base one or three feet distant from it.

THE DIFFERENT STYLES OF BATTING.

There are three styles of batting, in one or other of which every ball player more or less excels. The first is in holding the bat over the shoulder, as shown in the cut as follows :

(See cut on next page.)

The line of the bat in meeting the ball from this position forming a semi-circle. Second, in holding the bat forward with its point towards the first base and then drawing it back and swinging it forward to meet the ball as follows:

And third, in holding it back horizontally about hip-high, and swinging it on a level line to meet a hip-high ball, or on a semi-circular line to meet a low ball, as shown in the following cut :

In adapting either of the preceding styles, or, in fact, in regard to the adoption of any peculiar manner of holding the bat, habit is the principal guide, every batsman, as a general thing, finding it easier to hit the ball according to his own style than that of any other held up to him as a model. The best preparatory form for striking, however, is to stand as a backwoodsman does when using his axe in cutting down a tree, viz: poising the bat over the shoulder and standing in such form as to give the swing of the arm all the impetus a half twist of the body can impart to it. The style of holding the bat forward and then withdrawing it and swinging it forward again is a waste of strength, besides being a motion calculated to mar the aim of the striker. The holding of the bat horizontally and then making a double movement in striking is also objectionable, as wasting the strength of the wrists, whereas in holding it over the shoulder the weight of the bat, in coming down, is added to the impetus given it by the arms and body, besides affording the wrists a chance to assist the movement. In grasping the bat there are two methods in vogue, the one style being that in which the right hand holds the bat nearest the body, and the other in which the left hand grasps it nearest the body. In the one case the hands pull the bat to meet the ball, and in the other they push it. We incline to the opinion that the former is the most effective of the two. Muscular strength at the wrists has much to do with strong batting. We append the following cuts as an illustration : (*See cuts on next page.*)

THE BEST BALLS TO HIT.

There are four classes of balls pitched for the batsman to strike at, viz: Shoulder high, hip high, knee high and what are known as " low balls "—a ball about a foot from the ground. If you can swing a heavy bat handily, and are pretty accurate in your aim, a squarely-hit shoulder ball will clear the heads of the in-fielders and go too close to the ground to be easily caught on the fly by the out-fielders, but if you are not a sure hitter let this class of balls alone, as the chances are that you will tip out oftener than you

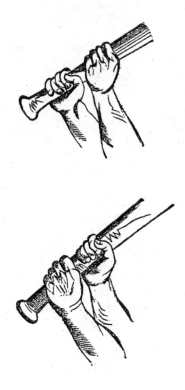

will get a square hit. Balls hip-high offer chances for good hits, provided the movement of the bat is timed well, and swung forward as near on a line with the ball as possible; but if the line of the bat forms a semi-circle in being swung forward, the chances are that the ball will either be missed or sent up in the air, and, of course, favorably for a catch. More ground balls are hit from knee high balls, than from any other class pitched; in fact, it must be a very poorly timed strike that would not send a knee-high ball skimming along the ground, about a foot or two from it, making it difficult to stop and almost impossible to catch. A low ball is only advantageous for strong hitters who can send a ball over the heads of the out-fielders, as there are not one out of ten of this class of balls that do not rise high when hit.

In timing these various balls, a shoulder ball is to be met by the bats according to the direction the batsman desires to send it ; if to the right field it should be met back of the base ; if to the left it must be met forward of the base, and the batsman, in taking his stand for the purpose of striking a ball to either one or the other of these positions, should either face the first-baseman or the short-stop according as he wants to send the ball to right or left fields. In thus facing for direction, however, the speed of the ball must be taken into consideration, for should the batsman face for a right-field ball, while swift balls are being pitched, and should the pitcher suddenly drop his pace a couple of yards, the striker would find his bat sending the ball square for the third baseman. In timing a hip-high ball for a grounder, the ball should be hit back of the home base, but if a hit to long field is intended, then the ball must be met over the home base or forward of it, according to the pace of the delivery. In timing knee-high balls, they must be invariably met back of the home base ; if forward of it, up they will go just the thing for fly catches.

BAD HABIT OF BATSMEN.

Some batsmen have a habit of slinging their bats behind

them as soon as they have hit the ball, without any regard as to whether they knock the catcher or Umpire down by the operation. All that is necessary for them to do when they have hit the ball is to *drop* the bat, not fling it from them. Another bad habit in vogue is, that of judging the character of the ball hit—some batsmen considering themselves Umpires in this respect. The moment a batsman hits a ball he should drop his bat and run for his base with all his speed. When he hears the Umpire call " foul " it is time enough for him to stop. The habit some have of stopping half way to the base, when they see a ball popped up, which affords an easy chance for a catch, or when they see the ball fielded by the pitcher or some in-fielder, and they think that it will go to the base sure, and that therefore there is no need of running, is a very foolish habit. There is nothing sure about base ball, and many an easy catch has been missed, and many a ball poorly fielded, by which the striker would have made his base had he continued running, when, by stopping, he has afforded the fielders a chance to make up for their error, by passing the ball to the base in time.

Being too particular in selecting a ball to strike at is poor policy. Make up your mind when you take your stand, to hit the first good ball that comes. The longer you wait the more hesitation there will be in your movements and the less accuracy of aim. We have seen batsmen wait fifteen minutes for a ball they wanted, and when the very ball came that they desired, they either failed to hit it at all, or struck so poorly that they were put out by it. Never wait for a man to leave his first base. In the first place you have no legal right to do so, and, secondly, you allow the pitcher a chance to play points on you, as we have shown in our article on pitching.

CHOOSING A BAT.

The lighter the bat, provided the wood is tough and elastic, the better, as a heavy bat, except, perhaps, in the hands of a strong-wristed man, mars the aim of the batsman in striking. Choose one that is well balanced, not top heavy. A well shaped bat tapers gradually from the point to the handle. Have it marked, so that you may strike the ball with one face of the bat, and that the least likely to break it. Have it full two and a half inches thick if it be a willow bat, but no other wood except pine will admit of this thickness and be light enough to handle well. In regard to length, the material of which the bat is made settles that point; if it be of light wood, forty inches is the best length; but if of hard wood from two to four inches shorter. The average of New York bats is thirty-eight inches; of Philadelphia forty inches; of Boston forty-two inches. Two and a half pounds is heavy for a good bat. A well seasoned ash bat is tough in fibre and has an elastic spring. Maple is a good wood for a heavy bat. Hickory, however, admits only of a length of thirty-six inches and two inches in diameter at most; it is the wood, however, for the bat of a strong man, with a quick eye, and practiced wrist. Hickory will admit of a thinner handle than any other wood.

Some new bats have recently been introduced which infringe the rule in reference to the bat, inasmuch as they are made with insertions of rubber or whalebone. Now the rule section 2—says that the bat "must be made of wood." All bats in which any material but wood forms a component part of the bat are not allowable in match games.

BASE BALL PRACTICE.

THE BENEFIT OF PRACTICE.

"PRACTICE makes perfect," is an old adage, but it is one specially applicable to base ball players. In cultivating the physical powers, certain preliminary exercises have to be gone through with, to reach any desired point of proficiency, but it should be borne in mind that these rudimental exercises are not to be thrown aside as soon as the required degree of proficiency has been achieved; on the contrary, they are important as a means of retaining the point of excellence attained. Thus the exercise of running the scales, practiced by a pianist, in cultivating the muscles of his hands, are as necessary in his daily exercises, when he has become a proficient in order to retain that proficiency, as they were as a means of learning him to play in the beginning. Just so is it in base ball. The exercise of throwing and catching being as necessary for the expert as the tyro. This fact, however, is ignored by many first class players, judging by their neglect of daily practice, and the result is, that when they come to play in a match they fail to reach the mark of playing skill, which characterized their fielding when in good training. The idea prevails among many players, who think they have reached the top of the ladder, that it is beneath their dignity to participate in the ordinary proceedings of a practice-day, and hence on such occasions, we frequently see this class of conceited men come on the field and "take a hand in," with an air of condescension as if they were conferring a favor by their presence. When a player has arrived at the point when he thinks himself the greatest player in the community, and thus "puts on airs," he ceases to be a valuable acquisition to any club. No player, no matter how skilled or experienced he may be, can afford to neglect practice, at least once a week, without feeling the effects of it in weakening his general play.

THE RIGHT KIND OF PRACTICE.

Base ball practice, to be really advantageous, should be regular and systematic. However beneficial, as regards rendering a player generally efficient, the ordinary mode of practice may be, it is not the method that should be adopted to make the first nine of a club perfect in all the departments of the game; nor is it adapted for acquiring individual proficiency. Let us see what this ordinary style of practice is. A club meets of an afternoon for practice.

As they come on the ground, dressed in their uniforms, first one and then another takes a bat in hand, and at it they go in batting the ball from one end of the field to the other. By this means they become expert in hitting a ball which *falls* to the bat; but for practice in hitting at *line* balls, as pitched to them, such practice is worse than useless. This thing done with, sides are chosen, and players are placed on bases whose forte is, perhaps, out-fielding, and others in the field who should be on the bases ; and what is more objectionable, the proficient and amateur get about the same amount of practice in the field, the former having but little good practice at the bat, the amateur, from lack of skill, gets less. As far as the fun of the thing is concerned this course may be well enough, although even in this respect a practice game of this kind is not as interesting either to players or spectators as one in which the skilled players are on one side in the irregular positions and a field side of amateurs on the other. Of course, a month of this kind of practice does not benefit the players as much as a few days of regular systematic training does. Now, by way of contrast, let us show the style of practice · adopted by a club who are aiming to make a nine that will whip the best in the country. When they come on the ground, if there are not enough to make up a party to fill the field, they man the bases and proceed to pass the ball around easily from one to another, first all round from base to base then across from first to third then to second and thence home, and so on, gradually increasing the pace of their throwing until the ball flies from hand to hand like a rifle shot. Either this is done or they throw the ball in from the outer-field, thereby practicing long throwing. Occasionally they vary this practice by quick, dodgy throws from one to another, first a high tossed ball, then a quick one to the ground, and so on, until a sufficient number are present to make up sides, when those of the first nine present take *their regular positions*, and, perhaps, seven of the nine will play against a field of ten, each man playing in his position with as much earnestness as in a match. This earnestness of play in practice is an important element in improving one's play. Laziness or indifference of manner, simply because it is only a practice game, retards rather than promotes advancement. It will readily be seen that there is a great difference between the two methods of practice, and the practical effect of each may be observed any day by watching the play of two clubs, the one of which practices in the old style—good enough for fun and exercise alone—and the other according to the plan adopted by clubs desirous of being the first players in the country.

HOW TO PRACTICE A NINE.

Every man of a first nine, besides being a good general player, capable of taking almost any position in the field in case of an emergency, should also be one competent to fill *one* position in the field better than he can any other, and whatever this one position is, it should be his post of duty on match days, and that, to the extent of being known in the club as " our first baseman," " our short-stop," " our catcher," pitcher, etc. This regular *home* position he should invariably occupy on such practice days, as the nine play together as a whole, in order that each player of the nine should make himself perfectly familiar with the peculiarities of play specially belonging to every position in a base ball field. Not one player in five thousand has the capacity to fill all positions ably and excel in each, the ability required being too great except for one like the admirable Creighton (not Crichton). But every man can excel in one position, and many in two or three. It is, therefore, advisable, and especially at an early period of the season, to make it a rule on practice days, when the first nine is pitted against the field, to place every fielder of the nine in his regular position. By this means a nine not only becomes thoroughly trained to play well into each others hands, but also to discharge the duties of each position in the most competent manner, and it is only by this systematic method of practice, together with the necessary attention to discipline, that a nine can ever attain that perfection of play which is calculated to place them in the front rank of the ball-playing community.

ON FIELDING.

FIELDING is the most attractive feature of a base ball match, and of all the requisites of a first nine player skill in fielding should be the primary qualifications demanded. "Muffins" can bat well, in a majority of cases, and occasionally we find one of this class who can pitch a pretty effective ball. Their lack of fielding skill, alone gives them the title of "muffins." Among the requisites of a first class fielder, are first, the moral qualifications of courage, nerve, control of temper and coolness of judgment in emergencies, together with perseverance in the face of difficulties and in contending manfully against large odds. The physical ability necessary, consists of the strength to throw a ball a hundred yards; the agility to catch a flying ball close to the ground, or two or three feet above your head; the activity to pick up a ball while running; the quickness of the eye to judge the fall of a high ball, or the rebound of a foul one, and the endurance to stand the fatigue of a long game. There are two classes of fielders, viz: out-fielders and in-fielders. The out-fielders are three, and the in-fielders six; the latter including the pitcher and catcher, short-stop and basemen. The whole of the fielders are called the "out hand" in the "field." We now proceed to describe the duties applicable to each position.

THE CATCHER'S POSITION.

Much of the success of a nine depends upon the ability of the catcher, and it is, therefore, requisite that he should be an excellent player in his position, and to excel as a catcher he should be able to throw with great accuracy and speed, a line ball a distance of fifty yards, and be able to stop swiftly-pitched balls and low grounders, and be especially on the alert in judging of foul-bound balls, besides having the nerve to face sharply-tipped balls direct from the bat. The ordinary rule is, when the striker has made his first base, for the catcher to come up close behind the bat in order to be in a position to take the ball from the pitcher quick enough to send it to second base, in case the base runner tries to steal a base on the pitcher. This rule does not work well in all cases however. It arose from the habit batsmen had, under the old rules, of waiting at the bat until a passed or overthrown ball had enabled the base runner to leave the first base—the pitcher and catcher formerly making it a regular point of play to pass the ball backward and forward to each other. This, however, is a custom that has been made obsolete by the new rules, and, therefore, the necessity of the catcher standing close behind the batsman is not as great as it used to be. The objection to the custom lays in the fact that it cramps the movements of the pitcher, as it obliges him to pitch for the catcher, in a measure, thereby, lessening his field for stratagetic play in pitching. The distance from the place the catcher stands to that occupied by the second baseman is not over fifty yards, and this is the greatest distance the catcher is required to throw in a game, and moving up behind the bat saves him but three or four yards in a throw. If possible, the catcher should be the captain of the nine, as from this position the best view of the field is to be had. The catcher and pitcher should always have a perfect understanding with each other in regard to their respective movements. Strategy is as important an element of success on a base ball field as on the field of battle. The pitcher and catcher should have a code of signals between them and they should practice these signs until they can read them as easily as their letters. Thus when the catcher sees an opportunity for the pitcher to catch a base player napping off his base, a certain signal should be given by which the pitcher may understand that he is to throw to the base promptly. Again, if the pitcher or the catcher are familiar with a certain habit of the batsman before them, of hitting at a favorite ball, the one who is acquainted with the batsman's weakness should give the other a sign informing him that he is going to send in a slower or swifter ball or a higher or lower one than ordinarily is pitched, or that such a change in the delivery is required from the pitcher by the catcher. Suppose, for instance, that the striker, who has either been put out, or has made his base, was one to whom swift balls had been sent, and that his successor is one whom slow balls bothers, the pitcher gives a sign to the catcher—one, of course, that cannot be observed by his opponents—to come up closer to the bat, thereby informing the catcher that he is going to drop his pace in delivery; the batsman not being aware of the proposed change prepares himself to meet the same class of balls which were pitched to the batsman preceding him, and the result is, that the change of pace leads him to strike too quick at the ball. Of course, if this change had been indicated to the batsman by the call of the pitcher to the catcher to stand up close behind for the change of pace, the batsman would have been placed upon his guard, and thereby would be prepared for the change; but this exposure of the design of the pitcher is prevented by the private signal and the judicious manner in which the change is carried out. Just so, too, is it when a change from slow to swift delivery is made, a private signal intimating to the catcher to get back for swift balls. The catcher too, should have a similar understanding with the out-fielders—who should watch him closely when a new batsman takes his stand at the home base—so that when any change of delivery by the pitcher is made, the catcher by a certain signal can either send the out-fielders farther out or closer in, according as the chances of a long high ball or a short one from the batsman are most probable. This stratagetic style of play is a great aid to success in all cases, but es-

pecially against inexperienced players, who do not perceive
the "nice little game" that is being played upon them:
When a catcher visits a new ground with his club, he
should avail himself of an hour's practice in catching foul
bound balls, in order to become familiar with the nature of
the ground in affecting the rebound of the ball, or otherwise, if he has been accustomed to catch on a lively ground
and plays on a dead one he will find his calculations for
catches behind on foul bounds rather out of the way. The
same, too, if he visits a lively ground after playing on a
dead field. The utmost good judgment in the catcher is
necessary in throwing to bases. Some catchers, who think
they throw a fine ball, make the mistake of throwing to all
three bases whenever the player runs to one or the other;
the result is, in most cases, that more bases are lost than if
no throws were made at all. First, be sure of your baseman; secondly, be sure of your aim; and thirdly, be sure
that you time your throw well, the latter being very important to the success of the movement. The catcher
should watch the movements of the fielders closely when a
high ball has been hit, so as to be ready to call out the name
of the fielder nearest the ball or most likely to catch it,
when two or more fielders are running to get it; and it
should be well understood that the moment the call is made
all the other fielders should stop running, or only prepare to
field the ball in case of a miss catch.

THE PITCHER'S POSITION.

We have referred to the duties of this position pretty
fully under the head of "Pitching," and, therefore, have
but little to remark further, beyond the fact, that the
pitcher requires to have the pluck, as a fielder, to face hot
balls from the bat, and to be on the alert in running to
bases to receive the ball from the party pitching it, in the
case of players returning to bases on foul or fly balls; and
also to be careful in watching the position of his men before
he handles the ball thrown to him after being struck foul,

for a sharp base runner will frequently steal a base on a pitcher, when the latter has handled the ball—viz : held it in his hands long enough to have been considered as settled— before the base player was in his position to receive it from the pitcher. He should have a thorough understanding with the catcher and out-fielders in regard to the code of signals adapted for a match, so that at any time he can either send the catcher further back or nearer in, when about to change his pace in delivery, or send out or draw in his out-fielders when about to pitch the batsman a ball for a catch.

THE POSITIONS OF THE BASEMEN.

There is quite a difference in the peculiarities of the position of the first baseman and those of the occupants of the other two bases, and also, as a matter of course, in regard to those appertaining to fielders, like the short-stop and the three out-fielders; hence, the importance of each man of the nine being specially familiar with the duties of the one position in which he is best calculated to play. For instance, the primary object of the first baseman is to hold the ball on the base before the striker reaches it; whereas, that of the second and third basemen is to touch players before reaching their bases. So, too, in regard to the difference between the duties of out-fielders and basemen— the latter requiring especially to be good throwers and catchers, while the forte of the basemen should be to hold swiftly-thrown balls, and to stop swiftly batted ones; the speciality of the short-stop being a combination of both features, with the addition of a special line of duty in supporting all the players of the in-field.

THE FIRST BASEMAN.

All basemen should be good ball catchers, but the occupant of the first base should specially excel in holding the swiftest thrown balls. He should, also, be fearless in facing hot balls from the bat, and expert in taking balls from the field, while holding one foot on the base. When a ball is hastily thrown to first base, his care should be to hold it, but at any rate to stop it. A good first base player ought to be able to hold a ball from the field, if it comes in anywhere within a radius of six feet from the base, and in case of high thrown balls he ought to take them, at least, eight feet high from the base. He must remember that the ball must be held by him—with some part of his person touching the base at the same time—before the striker reaches it, or the latter is not out; if the ball is held at the same time, the base runner is not out. When an overthrown ball to first base is stopped by the crowd in any way—accidentally or intentionally—he must first throw it to the pitcher's position before he can use it to put a player out; and also, that no ball hit by the batsman, on which a balk or a ball has been called, can put the striker out; no matter if held on the base in time, or caught on the fly or on a foul bound. Some first base players have a habit of taking their feet, or foot, off the base the moment the ball has been held, and this frequently leads them to do so before holding the ball, or so quickly as to look so to the Umpire, and the result is, that the striker is declared not out. In receiving a ball from the field, the first baseman should stand on the base in such a manner as not to prevent the runner from reaching his base, as the Umpire is justified in regarding any obstruction of the kind by the base player as intentional, if it could readily have been avoided, though the baseman may not have intended to obstruct his opponent, or prevent him from making his base except by legitimate means. In taking his position in the field, he should stand about twenty or thirty feet from the base towards the right field, and between the first and second bases, until the ball has been hit, when he should at once take his position with one foot on the first base, ready to receive the ball from the field. In taking his position for fielding, he will, of course, be guided by the style of batting opposed to him, standing further out in the field or closer to the base, according to the balls the batsman is in the habit of hitting. He should keep his eyes open for chances in points of play, especially when players are forced to vacate bases. Thus, for instance, suppose there is a player on the first base. when a ball is struck to the pitcher and held by him on the bound, should he forget to pass the ball to second base and send it to first base instead, the player standing on the base in the *interim* instead of running to the second base, the point of play for the basemen would be to take the ball from the pitcher while off the first base, and first touching the player standing on the base, put his foot on the base with ball in hand, thereby making a double play; for though the base runner was on the base when touched he had no legal right to be there, inasmuch as the batsman, not being put out, forced the base runner to leave the base, and he—the base runner—had no title to the first base until the batsman was put out. Had the baseman, in the above instance, touched the base first, with ball in hand, and then touched the player on it, the latter would not have been out, as, the moment the striker was put out the base runner ceased to be forced to leave the base. Similar points to this can frequently be made when a player is on the first base and the batsman hits a high ball, as the former in case the ball is caught has to return to first base, and in case it is missed is forced to leave for the second base and is, therefore, very likely to be put out there. A left hand player is the man for a first baseman; on any other base such a player is out of place.

THE SECOND BASEMAN.

The second baseman requires to be a pretty active fielder an accurate thrower for a short distance, and a pretty sure catch; he should, however, be very expert in catching a swiftly thrown ball and in holding it firmly and putting it quickly on the player running to his base. He is required to cover the second base and to play " right-short-stop " too; but his position in the field must be governed entirely by the style of batting he is called upon to face. If a strong hitter comes to the bat and swift balls are being sent in he should play well out in the field between right field and second base, and be on the *qui vive* for long bound balls, or high fly balls which drop between the out-field and the second base line. When the batsman makes his first base the second baseman comes up and gets near his base in readiness to receive the ball from the catcher. He should remember that in a majority of cases his duty is to touch the base runner and this it would be well to do in all cases when the latter is found off his base though in cases of foul balls, not yet returned to the pitcher, or when a ball has been stopped by the crowd and then thrown to second before being sent to the pitcher's position, no man can be put out by being touched when off his base. The habit, however, is a good one to get into, as there is then no likelihood of its being forgotten when it becomes necessary for a player to be touched. When the first baseman runs after the ball hit by the striker, the second baseman should at once make for the first base, as he is generally nearer to it than either the short-stop or pitcher when balls are being hit to first base. In timing for a throw to first base be sure of your aim, or if in doubt let the base be made, or otherwise the chances are that an overthrow will give your opponent his third instead of his first base. Hasty throwing is poor policy except you are pretty sure in sending in a swift line ball, and you have a good man at first base to hold it. When a player is on the first base, and another on the third, be on the watch so as to make a prompt return of the ball when the catcher throws to the second and the man on the third attempts to run home on the throw. There is ample time for a ball to be thrown from home to second and back to put out a player running home.

THE THIRD BASEMAN.

The third baseman's duties are the most onerous of the three positions on the bases, as on his good fielding will frequently depend the loss of runs to his opponents, when the failures on the other bases are only made at the cost of a single base. In the case of a miss play at third base, however, one or more runs scored is generally the result, that is, in cases where players are running their bases. When no men are on the bases the third basemen will have to be active in fielding the ball, and quick and accurate in throwing it, in order to prevent the striker from making his base. The third baseman takes a position closer to his base than either of the other baseman. Sometimes, however, he takes the place of the short-stop when the latter covers the second base in cases where the second baseman plays at right-short for a right-field hitter, a position frequently taken by a first class nine. In throwing from base to base hastily, take care that you throw low rather than high, as a low ball can be stopped if not handled, whereas a ball overhead gives a run on bases in nearly every instance. In fact, in the long run it is safer to allow a player to make one base than to run the risk of helping him to two or three bases by an overthrow. Accurate throwing from base to base is a pretty feature of the game, and with straight throwers and sure catchers can be safely indulged in at all times, for though a player may not be put out by a throw, when he sees the ball thrown straight and handed prettily it makes him hug his bases closer. Every base player should be active in "backing up" in the in-field. The life of fielding is in the support afforded each other by the fielders who are located near together. A good fielder or base player never stands still; he is always on the move ready for a spring to reach the ball, a stoop to pick it up, or a prompt movement to stop it, and he always has his eye upon the ball, especially when it is flying about inside the base lines or from base to base. Poor base players seldom put themselves out of the way to field a ball unless it comes within their special district, but a good base player is on the alert to play at a moment's notice, on any base from which the player has gone after the ball. When bases are vacated, or foul or fly balls are struck, all the base players handle the ball in the same way as at first base, but it is advisable to make sure always by touching the player when he is off the base.

THE SHORT-STOP'S POSITION.

The position of short-stop is the most important, as regards fielding, of any in the in-field. It is one requiring a very active player to discharge its duties properly. Especially is it incumbent on the short-stop to back up all the positions of the in-field. When a player has made his first base and is running to second on a throw from the catcher to the second base, the short-stop should run behind the second base to stop the ball in case the baseman should miss it. He should also back up the third baseman in the same way, and always be on hand to pick up a bound ball when missed on the fly by the third baseman or pitcher, or when it falls out of the reach of the party running after it on the fly. In the same way, too, should he support the pitcher in taking high balls on the fly so as to be ready to field them to the bases in case they are missed. No player is fitted to occupy this position who is not quick and lively in his movements in backing up all the position of the in-field. When a player is on the first base and one on the third, and the catcher holds the ball ready to throw to second, the short-stop should get nearly on the line of the pitcher and second baseman and have an understanding with the catcher to have him throw the ball to short-stop instead of second base, for on seeing the ball leave the catcher's hands apparently for second base, the player on the third will be apt to leave for home, in which case the short-stop will have the ball in hand ready to throw either to the catcher or third base; by this means, though the player running to second will have his base given him, the player on the third will be likely to be put out, and the player nearest home is the party to be put out first when there is any choice.

THE THREE OUT-FIELDERS.

The occupants of the three positions in the outer field,

viz : left, centre and right fields, should be equal in their qualifications as fielders. Each should be able to throw a ball a hundred yards, certainly not less than eighty at least. They should be good runners and excellent judges of fly balls. They should never stand still or occupy one position all the time, but be on the move ready for a quick run, or to back up each other. In judging of fly balls, it is always safer to lay out for a long hit, than to get so close in as to have to get back to catch a ball. They never should hold a ball a minute but return it to the infield as soon as handled. The point to throw the ball in to, is the pitcher's position, as a general thing, but as to that they will have to be guided by circumstances, according as the ball sent to them is taken on the fly, or fielded while a player is running his bases. One or other of the positions in the outer-field is the place for the changed pitcher of the nine, as it will afford him a chance to rest. The outfielders should watch the movements of the pitcher and catcher closely whenever a new batsman takes his stand at the home base, in order to be ready to obey any signals either to come in or to go out further, according to the character of the pitching or the peculiar style of the batsman.

GENERAL HINTS ON FIELDING.

There is no habit fielders have, that is more characteristic of school boys, or which leads to more unpleasantness and ill-feeling in a match, than that of finding fault with those who commit errors of play in the field. Every man in the field tries to do his best for his own credit sake, and if he fails censure but adds to his chagrin without in the least improving his play; on the contrary, fault-finding is only calculated to make him play worse. In no game are the amenities of social life more necessary to a full enjoyment of the pastime than in base ball. Particularly acceptable are words of commendation for good play, and remarks calculated to remove the annoyance arising from errors in the field, to young ball players, and these form some of the strongest incentives to extra exertion on their part, besides promoting kindly feelings on the field and during the game. We must enter our protest against the fault-finding, grumbling and snarling dispositions which continually censures every failure to succeed, and barely tolerates any creditable effort that does not emanate from themselves or in which they do not participate. Such men as these constitutional grumblers are the nuisances of a ball field, and destroy all the pleasure which would otherwise result from the game. Every manly player will keep silent when he sees an error committed, or if he makes any remark at all, will apologize for it in some way. Those who find fault and growl at errors of play are of the class who prefer to gratify their malice and ill-temper at the expense of the unlucky fielder who happens to " muff " a ball or two in a game.

Fielders should remember that the captain of the nine is alone the spokesman of the party and the commander of the field.

No out-fielder should hold a ball a moment longer than it is necessary for him to handle it in throwing. In the infield, however, a ball can be sometimes held by the fielder with safety and advantage.

Never stand still in your position simply because the ball happens to go in another direction than the position you occupy, but always be on the move to aid the other fielders or to back them up. Activity in the field and judgment in being prompt in support is the characteristic of a first class fielder.

Play earnestly at all times, whether in an ordinary practice game or in a match. Get into the habit of doing your best on all occasions. It is invariably the mark of a vain and conceited ball player to walk on the field and play in a game as if he was conferring a favor by participating in the game; and players who play with an air of indifference as to the result of the game, or who become despondent when the odds are against them are no players for a first class nine.

Next to seeing a man field well, the most attractive thing is to see a player take things easy and good naturedly. If you miss a fly ball, allow an important ball to pass you, or fail to handle a ball in time on a base, nothing is more boyish than to vent your ill-temper on some one who may have balked you in catching it, or thrown it to you badly. Control yourself and take it smilingly, or if you lack the moral courage to do that keep your mouth shut at least. Your good-natured fellows who play their best all the time, and yet take everything bad or good with a good-natured smile, are as desirable as companions on a ball field as your growlers are to be detested.

When an error of play is committed do your best at once to remedy the evil by using your best efforts to get at the ball either after missing it, letting it pass you, or failing to hold it. Some players after " muffing " a ball will walk after it like an ill-tempered, sulky ten-year old.

Remember that the winning of the trophy is one of the main objects in view, and as it is not the most important thing in life to win it, or a very great disaster to lose it, the less you act as if it was, the less likelihood of the spectators suspecting you of having some ulterior object in view, such as the winning of a sum of money for instance. Playing for money we believe is something not quite unknown in base ball, we regret to say. To conclude, however, let it be remembered by every player in a match that a *creditable* victory abides only with that party, who, in winning the match, have marked their play as much by their courtesy of demeanor, liberality of action and the good nature they have displayed in the contest, as by their skill in the several departments of the game.

PLAYING BASE BALL ON THE ICE.

Playing base ball on the ice differs from the field game in regard to the form of the bases and the method of running them. The ordinary rules governing the batsman and pitcher too, are not so strictly observed as in the field game,

the impossibility of obtaining a good footing making the
operation of pitching and batting rather difficult.   In running the bases in a game on the ice on skates, all that is
necessary for the base runner to do is to cross the line of
the position, after which he cannot be put out until he has
returned to the base, and again leaves it.   In order, too,
to make the succeeding base he must cross the base line in
starting from the base he leaves as well as the line of the
base he runs for.   The following is a diagram of the base
lines for a game on the ice, the lines being marked by some
dark coloring matter not likely to soil the clothes as paint
does :

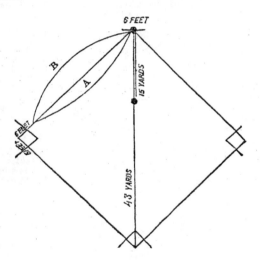

The base lines are laid down on the ice so as to enclose a space of three feet square, each line being marked at right angles with the base lines from base to base, and three feet each side thereof. This space forms the base, and within this space the base player must have some part of his person when he holds the ball, in order to put a player out. The base runner makes his base if he *crosses the line of the base* before being touched, or before the ball is held on the base. After hitting a ball on which the batsman can only make one base, he should start from the home base so as to turn to the right as shown by line A in crossing the lines of the base; but in cases where his hit entitles him to two or more bases then he should start so as to turn to the left, as shown by line B. Until he has returned and occupied a base after crossing the line in making it, he cannot be put out.

Were the regular bases used in games on the ice and the rules of the field game observed, the effort of players to stop suddenly would lead to severe falls, and, therefore, the extended lines for bases are used, and the rules changed to conform to the new line.

In match games on the ice ten men are usually selected, the tenth man playing at right-short field. Five innings only are generally played.

TECHNICAL TERMS TO BASE BALL.

A LINER.—A ball sent swift and straight from the bat without rising in the air; or one thrown similarly to a base.

A HOT ONE.—A very swiftly thrown or batted ball.

A MUFFED BALL.—A ball which the fielder touches but fails to hold or stop.

A GROUNDER.—A ball hit along the ground, either on a line or on a series of bounds. (A telling hit at all times as it invariably secures a base.)

A DAISY CUTTER.—A line ball sent close to the ground and cutting through the grass.

DROPPING THE PACE.—Sending in a slow ball suddenly after having pitched swiftly for some time.

FACING FOR DIRECTION.—Standing at the home base with the bat, and facing the fielder towards whose position in the field you desire to send the ball.

FORCED FROM A BASE.—You are forced to leave a base either when all are occupied, and you stand on any one of the bases when the striker hits a fair ball, or when you are on the first base and a fair ball is struck.

FUNGOES.—A preliminary practice game in which one player takes the bat and tossing the ball up hits it as it falls, and if the ball is caught in the field, on the fly, the player catching it takes the bat. It is useless as practice in batting, but good for taking fly balls.

POPPING ONE UP.—Hitting a ball up in the air over the head of the pitcher or in-fielders so that it can be readily caught by any of them.

ONE, TWO, THREE.—Another preliminary practice game in which all the positions of the field are occupied alternately. Thus, for instance, the striker hits a ball and is put out, he goes to the out-field, the catcher takes the bat, the pitcher goes behind, the first baseman goes in to pitch, the 2d goes to 1st, 3d to 2d, short to 1st, left to short-stop centre to left and right to centre. If the ball is hit and the striker makes his bases and comes in he bats in turn in the place of the catcher, in which case each player retains his position until the next player is put out. By this means every player on the field occupies in turn every position on the field.

THE IN-FIELD.—That portion of the field within the base lines. The in-fielders include the first six players of a nine beginning with the catcher and ending with the short-stop.

THE OUT-FIELD.—The out-fielders are the left centre and right-field positions.

TIMING A BALL.—To time a ball well is to hit it in the centre and in such a manner as to send it in the very direction you want it to go. Thus, for instance, in timing a knee-high ball sent in swiftly to the bat, the striker should time the swing of his bat for a grounder so as to meet the ball back of the base; and for a hit to long field he should meet the ball just over the base or a little forward of it. The pace of the pitching must be taken into consideration in timing the swing of the bat.

RUN OUT.—A player is "run out," when he is caught between two bases and is put out by one or other of the fielders.

PASSED BALLS.—A passed ball is one muffed by the catcher on which a base is run.

AN OVER-PITCH.—A ball pitched over the head of the catcher on which bases are made.

A WILD THROW.—A ball thrown over the head of a baseman or the catcher on which bases are made.

A HOME RUN.—A run made from home to home from a hit to long-field, the player going from base to base without stopping before the ball reaches the catcher

THE END.

CONTENTS.

APPENDIX.

Note for Page 16.

If the batsman, almost simultaneously with the Umpire's call of "three balls" hits the called ball, and it be caught on the fly, the Striker is not out, and, moreover, he can take his first base on the third ball just the same as if he had not hit the ball; and so, also, can any base player, occupying a base at the same time, take a base on the third ball called. In case of a baulked ball hit by the striker and caught on the fly, however, though the striker is not out, he cannot take a base on the baulk because he is not a player running the base; but any player occupying a base can take a base on the baulked ball. Umpires should study the bearings of this rule well, for though easily interpreted when perfectly understood, a cursory glance at it would lead to some confusion of ideas in defining it. The principle of the rule, however, is that no player can be put out on a hit baulked or dead ball, and that neither can a base player take a base on a dead ball except according to such specifications as appear in rule six. If a player desires to risk or attempt to run on a base or a dead ball he can do so, but he cannot be given one on such a ball unless as provided in rule No. 6. It should also be borne in mind that if the striker hit a dead ball foul the Umpire is not to call foul, as the striker cannot legitimately hit a ball foul unless he striks at a fair ball.

Note for Page 26.

The change referred to here means the substitution of one player in the nine for another, and does not refer to any changes made in the positions of the nine players, for the rules do not in any way prohibit changes in the positions of any of the nine players in the field, for the Captain of a nine has the power to change the position in the field of any man of the nine, thus taking the first baseman from his base and placing in the outer field, or making the catcher the pitcher or *vice versa*.

HANDBOOK OF VENTRILOQUISM.

This little work, though only recently published, has met with an extensive sale, and the testimony of readers and the press fully sustains our claim that it is the best treatise on the subject that has been published. In all previous publications purporting to treat this subject, there has been really very little practical information given; and though perhaps in some cases readable enough, the main object which the purchaser desired, instruction in the art, was not attained. The instructions in the present volume are very plain and minute, founded on common sense, and by their aid any one with patience and practise may become a ventriloquist, as the learner, after a few lessons, is able to exercise this power in some measure. The course of study and practice is by no means disagreeable or tiresome. The book also gives instructions for making

THE MAGIC WHISTLE,

A little instrument easily made, at no cost, for imitating birds, animals, insects, and quite a number of other amusing imitations. Considerable practice is required to enable one to use the whistle satisfactorily. The entertainment to be derived from it, however, will amply repay the labor.

" It is really a valuable aid to those desirous of acquiring the art, and the instructions and explanations are so simple and explicit that there is no difficulty in understanding them. It is prepared with much more care than we should expect in such a low-priced work, and makes a handy pocket companion.' "—*Boston Wide World.*

" This little manual contains simple and explicit instructions for acquiring the art of ventriloquism. Couched in language which a child can understand, the rules are so few and so easy that a little practice will enable any one to procure the most wonderful vocal illusions."—*New York Atlas.*

" The author appears to have labored faithfully to explain the mysteries of the art, and to initiate the learner therein."—*Yankee Blade.*

☞ This, and all other works in our list, will be sent post paid on receipt of price.

Price Fifteen Cents.